LifeChange

S E R I E S

A NavPress Bible study on the book of

PROVERBS

NAVPRESS®

Bringing Truth to Life

OUR GUARANTEE TO YOU

We believe so strongly in the message of our books that we are making this quality guarantee to you. If for any reason you are disappointed with the content of this book, return the title page to us with your name and address and we will refund to you the list price of the book. To help us serve you better, please briefly describe why you were disappointed. Mail your refund request to: NavPress, P.O. Box 35002, Colorado Springs, CO 80935.

The Navigators is an international Christian organization. Our mission is to reach, disciple, and equip people to know Christ and to make Him known through successive generations. We envision multitudes of diverse people in the United States and every other nation who have a passionate love for Christ, live a lifestyle of sharing Christ's love, and multiply spiritual laborers among those without Christ.

NavPress is the publishing ministry of The Navigators. NavPress publications help believers learn biblical truth and apply what they learn to their lives and ministries. Our mission is to stimulate spiritual formation among our readers.

www.navpress.com

NAVPRESS, BRINGING TRUTH TO LIFE, and the NAVPRESS logo are registered trademarks of NavPress. Absence of ® in connection with marks of NavPress or other parties does not indicate an absence of registration of those marks.

ISBN 08910-93486

Unless otherwise identified, all Scripture quotations in this publication are taken from the *Holy Bible: New International Version*® (NIV®). Copyright © 1973, 1978, 1984 by International Bible Society. Used by permission of Zondervan Publishing House. All rights reserved. Other versions used include: the *New American Standard Bible* (NASB), The Lockman Foundation 1960, 1962, 1963, 1968, 1971, 1972, 1973, 1975, 1977; and the *King James Version* (KJV).

Printed in the United States of America

18 19 20 21 22 23 24 25 / 10 09 08 07 06 05 04

FOR A FREE CATALOG OF NAVPRESS BOOKS & BIBLE STUDIES
CALL 1-800-366-7788 (USA) or 1-416-499-4615 (CANADA)

CONTENTS

ACKNOWLEDGMENTS

The LIFECHANGE series has been produced through the coordinated efforts of a team of Navigator Bible study developers and NavPress editorial staff, along with a nationwide network of fieldtesters.

AUTHOR: RON RHODES
SERIES EDITOR: KAREN LEE-THORP

HOW TO USE THIS STUDY

Objectives

Most guides in the LIFECHANGE series of Bible studies cover one book of the Bible. Although the LIFECHANGE guides vary with the books they explore, they share some common goals:

1. To provide you with a firm foundation of understanding and a thirst to return to the book;

2. To teach you by example how to study a book of the Bible without structured guides;

3. To give you all the historical background, word definitions, and explanatory notes you need, so that your only other reference is the Bible;

4. To help you grasp the message of the book as a whole;

5. To teach you how to let God's Word transform you into Christ's image.

Each lesson in this study is designed to take 60 to 90 minutes to complete on your own. The guide is based on the assumption that you are completing one lesson per week, but if time is limited you can do half a lesson per week or whatever amount allows you to be thorough.

Flexibility

LIFECHANGE guides are flexible, allowing you to adjust the quantity and depth of your study to meet your individual needs. The guide offers many optional questions in addition to the regular numbered questions. The optional questions, which appear in the margins of the study pages, include the following:

Optional Application. Nearly all application questions are optional; we hope you will do as many as you can without overcommitting yourself.

For Thought and Discussion. Beginning Bible students should be able to handle these, but even advanced students need to think about them. These questions frequently deal with ethical issues and other biblical principles. They often offer cross-references to spark thought, but the references do not give obvious answers. They are good for group discussions.

For Further Study. These include: a) cross-references that shed light on a topic the book discusses, and b) questions that delve deeper into the passage. You can omit them to shorten a lesson without missing a major point of the passage.

If you are meeting in a group, decide together which optional questions to prepare for each lesson, and how much of the lesson you will cover at the next meeting. Normally, the group leader should make this decision, but you might let each member choose his or her own application questions.

As you grow in your walk with God, you will find the LIFECHANGE guide growing with you—a helpful reference on a topic, a continuing challenge for application, a source of questions for many levels of growth.

Overview and Details

The study begins with an overview of the book of Proverbs. The key to interpretation is context—what is the whole passage or book *about?*—and the key to context is purpose—what is the author's *aim* for the whole work? In lesson one you will lay the foundation for your study of Proverbs by asking yourself, "Why did the author (and God) write the book? What did they want to accomplish? What is the book about?"

In lessons one through fourteen you will analyze passages of Proverbs in detail.

In lesson fifteen you will review Proverbs, returning to the big picture to see whether your view of it has changed after closer study. Review will also strengthen your grasp of major issues and give you an idea of how you have grown from your study.

Kinds of Questions

Bible study on your own—without a structured guide—follows a progression. First you observe: What does the passage *say?* Then you interpret: What does the passage *mean?* Lastly you apply: How does this truth *affect* my life?

Some of the "how" and "why" questions will take some creative thinking, even prayer, to answer. Some are opinion questions without clear-cut right answers; these will lend themselves to discussions and side studies.

Don't let your study become an exercise of knowledge alone. Treat the passage as God's Word, and stay in dialogue with Him as you study. Pray, "Lord, what do You want me to see here?" "Father, why is this true?" "Lord, how does this apply to my life?"

It is important that you write down your answers. The act of writing clarifies your thinking and helps you to remember.

Study Aids

A list of reference materials, including a few notes of explanation to help you make good use of them, begins on page 145. This guide is designed to include enough background to let you interpret with just your Bible and the guide. Still, if you want more information on a subject or want to study a book on your own, try the references listed.

Scripture Versions

Unless otherwise indicated, the Bible quotations in this guide are from the New International Version of the Bible. Other versions cited are the New American Standard Bible (NASB) and the King James Version (KJV).

Use any translation you like for study, preferably more than one. A paraphrase such as The Living Bible is not accurate enough for study, but it can be helpful for comparison or devotional reading.

Memorizing and Meditating

A psalmist wrote, "I have hidden your word in my heart that I might not sin against you" (Psalm 119:11). If you write down a verse or passage that challenges or encourages you, and reflect on it often for a week or more, you will find it beginning to affect your motives and actions. We forget quickly what we read once; we remember what we ponder.

When you find a significant verse or passage, you might copy it onto a card to keep with you. Set aside five minutes during each day just to think about what the passage might mean in your life. Recite it over to yourself, exploring its meaning. Then, return to your passage as often as you can during your day, for a brief review. You will soon find it coming to mind spontaneously.

For Group Study

A group of four to ten people allows the richest discussions, but you can adapt this guide for other sized groups. It will suit a wide range of group types, such as home Bible studies, growth groups, youth groups, and businessmen's studies. Both new and experienced Bible students, and new and mature Christians, will benefit from the guide. You can omit or leave for later years any questions you find too easy or too hard.

The guide is intended to lead a group through one lesson per week. However, feel free to split lessons if you want to discuss them more thoroughly. Or, omit some questions in a lesson if preparation or discussion time is limited. You can always return to this guide for personal study later. You will be able to discuss only a few questions at length, so choose some for discussion and others for background. Make time at each discussion for members to ask about anything they didn't understand.

Each lesson in the guide ends with a section called "For the group." These sections give advice on how to focus a discussion, how you might apply the lesson in your group, how you might shorten a lesson, and so on. The group leader should read each "For the group" at least a week ahead so that he or she can tell the group how to prepare for the next lesson.

Each member should prepare for a meeting by writing answers for all of the background and discussion questions to be covered. If the group decides not to take an hour per week for private preparation, then expect to take at least two meetings per lesson to work through the questions. Application will be very difficult, however, without private thought and prayer.

Two reasons for studying in a group are accountability and support. When each member commits in front of the rest to seek growth in an area of life, you can pray with one another, listen jointly for God's guidance, help one another to resist temptation, assure each other that the other's growth matters to you, use the group to practice spiritual principles, and so on. Pray about one another's commitments and needs at most meetings. Spend the first few minutes of each meeting sharing any results from applications prompted by previous lessons. Then discuss new applications toward the end of the meeting. Follow such sharing with prayer for these and other needs.

If you write down each other's applications and prayer requests, you are more likely to remember to pray for them during the week, ask about them at the next meeting, and notice answered prayers. You might want to get a notebook for prayer requests and discussion notes.

Notes taken during discussion will help you to remember, follow up on ideas, stay on the subject, and clarify a total view of an issue. But don't let note-taking keep you from participating. Some groups choose one member at each meeting to take notes. Then someone copies the notes and distributes them at the next meeting. Rotating these tasks can help include people. Some groups have someone take notes on a large pad of paper or erasable marker board (preformed shower wallboard works well), so that everyone can see what has been recorded.

Pages 148-149 list some good sources of counsel for leading group studies. The *Small Group Letter*, published by NavPress, is unique, offering insights from experienced leaders every other month.

INTRODUCTION

The Book of Proverbs

As Psalms is the hymnbook of the Old Testament, so Proverbs is its teacher's manual. The moral maxims found there were used in ancient Israel to help the young acquire mental skills that promote wise living. Both the *content* of the proverbs and their *structure* contributed to the students' development.

The word *proverb* comes from a verb meaning "to be like, to be compared with, to be parallel, to be similar."[1] Hence, a proverb is simply a form of communicating truth by using comparisons or figures of speech. As brief maxims, the proverbs crystallize and condense the writers' experiences and observations. The concentrated sayings cause the reader to chew on them until the truth is extracted and digested. The reward for this effort is wisdom.

Wisdom and skillful living

Wisdom is the theme that weaves through the book of Proverbs. The main Hebrew word for wisdom is *hokmah*. It was used commonly for the skill of craftsmen, sailors, singers, administrators, and counselors.[2] *Hokmah* pointed to the experience and efficiency of these various workers in using their skills.

Similarly, a person who possesses *hokmah* in his spiritual life and relationship to God is one who is both knowledgeable and experienced in following God's way. Biblical wisdom essentially involves skill in the art of godly living.

Jewish teachers realized that "wise living requires the ability to reach sound decisions and to make the right choices, and thus the *ability to discriminate* between what is right and what is wrong, wholesome and damaging, important and unimportant, wise and foolish."[3] The attainment of *hokmah* was accordingly a high priority (which in turn made the study of Proverbs a high priority).

The wisdom of Solomon

Scholars agree that the majority of the proverbs were written by Solomon.[4] He was a man of outstanding wisdom (1 Kings 3), and his court became an international center for the exchange of wisdom and learning. First Kings 4:29-34 tells us,

> God gave Solomon wisdom and very great insight, and a breadth of understanding as measureless as the sand on the seashore. Solomon's wisdom was greater than the wisdom of all the men of the East, and greater than all the wisdom of Egypt. He was wiser than any other man . . . and his fame spread to all the surrounding nations. He spoke three thousand proverbs, and his songs numbered a thousand and five. . . . Men of all nations came to listen to Solomon's wisdom, sent by all the kings of the world, who had heard of his wisdom.

Solomon's great wisdom was given to him as a result of a request he made to God. While at Gibeon (where the Tabernacle stood), Solomon had sacrificed a thousand burnt offerings. Then God showed His pleasure by appearing to Solomon in a dream, inviting him to make a request. Solomon humbly requested wisdom to rule the Israelites. Here is how God responded to that request:

> Since you have asked for this and not for long life or wealth for yourself, nor have asked for the death of your enemies but for discernment in administering justice, I will do what you have asked. I will give you a wise and discerning heart, so that there will never have been anyone like you, nor will there ever be. (1 Kings 3:11-12)

To augment his own personal wisdom from God, Solomon also collected and edited many proverbs that he did not author himself. Ecclesiastes tells us that Solomon studied, weighed, and arranged proverbs (Ecclesiastes 12:9). Proverbs existed before Solomon's time (Numbers 21:27, 1 Samuel 24:13), and many have been discovered in the literature of countries surrounding Israel.[5] Nevertheless, as the author of three thousand proverbs, Solomon's wisdom was unparalleled. Truly, he was a master of *hokmah*, and as we study Proverbs, he is our mentor.

Hebrew poetry

The book of Proverbs is written entirely in poetry. Since Hebrew poetry is constructed differently from English, it helps to know some of the ground rules.

English poetry is based on rhythm and rhyme. Hebrew poetry doesn't rhyme, and its rhythm is hard to imitate in translation. Instead, the main structural feature of Hebrew poetry is called *parallelism* or *intensification*. That is, the lines in each verse are parallel in some way, so that the second line somehow intensifies the meaning of the first. (If there are three lines, the third intensifies more, and so on.)

10

For example, in *synonymous parallelism*, the concepts in the first line are paralleled by similar concepts in the second line. Proverbs 2:11 says,

Discretion will protect you,
and understanding will guard you.

This does not mean that discretion equals understanding. The two lines are not identical in meaning ("synonymous" is a somewhat misleading label). Rather, the lines look at different facets of a larger truth. They build on each other.

In *antithetical parallelism*, the second line is the opposite of (or in contrast with) the first. Proverbs 10:1 says,

A wise son brings joy to his father,
but a foolish son grief to his mother.

This is not to say that a foolish son doesn't grieve his father. Rather, the second line looks at the truth of the first from another angle, thereby intensifying it and driving it home.

In *emblematic parallelism*, one line illustrates or clarifies the other with a word picture. Proverbs 10:26 reads,

As vinegar to the teeth and smoke to the eyes,
so is a sluggard to those who send him.

Finally, in *synthetic parallelism*, the second line simply continues the same thought of the first. It may tell the result of what the first line mentions, as in Proverbs 3:6:

In all your ways acknowledge him,
and he will make your paths straight.

Or, the second line may describe something mentioned in the first, as in Proverbs 15:3:

The eyes of the LORD are everywhere,
keeping watch on the wicked and the good.

Proverbs and daily life

The book of Proverbs adds an important dimension to the Old Testament. It is conceivable that a Jew could be in complete obedience to the Law of Moses, yet he still might not be leading a full life. The book of Proverbs meets this need by setting forth a skillful approach to daily living. It might be considered God's book on "how to wise up and live." It applies God's principles to the whole of life . . . to relationships, the home, work, justice, decisions, attitudes, reactions, everything a man says and even thinks.

Old Testament scholar Derek Kidner tells us that "the samples of behav-

11

ior which it [Proverbs] holds up to view are all assessed by one criterion, which could be summed up in the question, 'Is this wisdom or folly?'"[6] The answer to this question in each situation determines what action to take.

"There is calculation in Proverbs," says Kidner, "for there is every encouragement to count the cost or reward of one's actions, and to study the ways of getting things done; but wisdom as taught here is God-centred, and even when it is most down-to-earth it consists in the shrewd and sound handling of one's affairs in *God's* world, in submission to *His* will."[7]

It is important to note that the proverbs are not intended to be *promises* that are invariably true without exception. They are *general principles* or *guidelines* that are usually but not always true. The books of Job and Ecclesiastes were written to correct people who believed that such teachings of wisdom as "the righteous will be healthy and wealthy, the wicked will die young" were iron-clad laws. The overall message of Scripture is that the proverbs are true enough to live your life by, and that God always has wise reasons when He makes exceptions.

Modern relevance

The book of Proverbs is as relevant today as it was in 700 BC when it was completed. Though times have changed, people are essentially the same. They have the same needs and desires, the same fears, problems, temptations, and ultimate goals. Furthermore, since God inspired the authors of the book to record what they did, the wisdom they wrote is timeless. Any twentieth-century believer who wants to become skilled in the art of godly living (to gain *hokmah*) will find his desire fulfilled in studying Proverbs.

1. *Theological Wordbook of the Old Testament*, edited by R. Laird Harris, Gleason L. Archer, Jr., and Bruce K. Waltke, volume 1 (Chicago: Moody Press, 1980), page 533.
2. *Nelson's Expository Dictionary of the Old Testament*, edited by Merrill F. Unger and William White (Nashville: Thomas Nelson Publishers, 1980), pages 473-475.
3. Kenneth T. Aitken, *Proverbs* (Philadelphia: The Westminster Press, 1986), page 11.
4. Sid S. Buzzell, "Proverbs," *The Bible Knowledge Commentary* (Wheaton: Victor Books, 1985), page 901.
5. Norman L. Geisler, *A Popular Survey of the Old Testament* (Grand Rapids: Baker Book House, 1978), page 205.
6. Derek Kidner, *The Proverbs: An Introduction and Commentary* (Downers Grove: InterVarsity Press, 1964), page 13.
7. Kidner, pages 13-14.

PART I

Foundations:
Wisdom Versus Folly

PROVERBS 1:1-7, 1:20-2:10

Wisdom's Benefits

The opening chapters of Proverbs are meant to motivate us to study the book and introduce what the proverbs are about. Ask God to give you understanding as you study these first passages.

The beginning of knowledge (1:1-7)

Read 1:1-7.

1. Verse 1 identifies King Solomon as the primary author of the book. What do you learn from the following passages about the authors of some of the book's sections?

   30:1 _____

   _____

   31:1 _____

   _____

   _____

Men of Hezekiah (25:1). These were scribes (secretaries) of King Hezekiah, who lived about 250 years after Solomon. (Solomon reigned 970-930 BC, and Hezekiah reigned 715-686 BC. Isaiah lived during Hezekiah's reign.) These scribes

15

compiled additional proverbs from Solomon's repertoire and listed them in chapters 25-29. These same scribes may also have added the proverbs of Agur and Lemuel at that time. Proverbs 22:17 and 24:23 mention "the sayings of the wise," which Solomon or the scribes may have collected.

Acquiring (1:3). (NASB: "receive.") This word was used for plucking grapes and taking them for personal consumption.

Prudence (1:4). "Good judgment," "good sense."[1]

Discretion (1:4). The ability to plan ahead and plot a course of action with foresight.

Simple (1:4). A person who is "naive" (NASB) and untaught. "He is not an imbecile, one who cannot comprehend, or a fool who despises wisdom. Instead, he is one whose exposure to life and wisdom has been limited. Because of inexperience he is gullible and easily influenced."[2]

Guidance (1:5). (NASB: "counsel.") Literally, "steerings." The word has to do with moving one's life in the right direction.

2. What five purposes for Proverbs do you see in 1:2-6?

1:2a _____

_____

1:2b _____

_____

1:3 _____

_____

1:4-5 _____

_____

1:6 _____

_____

16

Beginning (1:7). The first and controlling principle, the essence. Possibly also the first step toward.

Fools (1:7). Unlike the simple, who are too inexperienced to understand wisdom, fools actively hate and avoid wisdom (1:22). The simple are on the fence, with the potential to become wise if they make the effort or fools if they choose not to.

3. Proverbs 1:7 states the theme of the book. How do people display "the fear of the LORD" in the following passages?

Exodus 20:18-21 _____

_____

_____

_____

_____

Joshua 2:1-14 _____

_____

_____

_____

_____

Job 1:1,4-5 _____

_____

_____

_____

_____

For Thought and Discussion: The fear of the Lord is the beginning of knowledge (1:7) and of wisdom (9:10). Do you think knowledge and wisdom are essentially the same, or is there a distinction? Explain.

Optional Application:
a. Would you say your lifestyle shows that you really fear God in a healthy sense? Why or why not?
b. How can you grow in this area?

17

Psalm 112:1, 128:1 _____

_____

_____

_____

_____

4. In light of these cross-references, how would you define "the fear of the LORD"?

_____

_____

_____

_____

_____

5. Why do you suppose this is the essence of or first step toward true knowledge?

_____

_____

_____

_____

_____

Warnings against rejecting wisdom
(1:20-33)

Study Skill—Personification
Personification is "a rhetorical figure of speech in which inanimate objects or abstractions are endowed with human qualities or are represented as possessing human form."[3] In Proverbs, wisdom is often personified as a woman.

Gateways (1:21). The city gateway was the normal place where the city's leaders met to conduct official business.

6. Read 1:20-33. How accessible is wisdom for those who really seek it (1:20-21)?

_____

_____

_____

Mockers (1:22). (NASB: "scoffers.") Proud, arrogant people who are self-opinionated and full of insults and contempt.

7. Observe how each of the three groups in 1:22 displays a lack of wisdom. What do they have in common?

_____

_____

_____

_____

_____

Rebuke (1:23). (NASB: "reproof.") A helpful kind of verbal correction. Solomon uses this word often, and he doesn't have in mind cutting remarks.

8. How are the ways of wisdom and folly contrasted in 1:32-33?

_____

_____

For Thought and Discussion: Why do you think Solomon chose to personify wisdom as a woman so often (3:16-18, 4:3-6, 8:1-21, 9:1-6, 14:33)?

Optional Application: Accepting rebuke is a major virtue in Proverbs (3:11, 9:8, etc.). How are you at accepting rebuke?

For Thought and Discussion: Proverbs 1:33 says those who heed wisdom will "live in safety." What about those godly Christians who suffer car accidents, violent crimes, and so on? Do these events prove 1:33 is wrong?

For Thought and Discussion: Why is it wise to pray passionately for wisdom? (See also 2 Chronicles 1:10, Psalm 90:12, Ephesians 1:17, Colossians 1:9, James 1:6.)

Optional Application: Design a short prayer for wisdom and record it on a 3 x 5 card. You might want to begin the rest of your studies of Proverbs with this prayer.

For Thought and Discussion: What are the benefits of memorizing Scripture (2:1-5)?

The fear of the Lord (2:1-10)

> **Study Skill—Paraphrasing**
> Restating a verse in your own words is often a good way to ensure that you understand what the author is saying. This is especially helpful for proverbs, which are pithy but concentrated and sometimes elusive. When in doubt, check other translations of the Bible or ask a mature Christian to check your paraphrase for accuracy.

Heart (2:2). The Hebrew word refers to the core of us where we think, feel, choose, and believe basic beliefs. It is often translated "mind," so we shouldn't think of the heart just as the place of emotions.

9. According to 2:1-5, how can one understand "the fear of the LORD"?

If (2:1-2) _____

_____

_____

If (2:3) _____

_____

_____

If (2:4) _____

_____

_____

20

Knowledge of God (2:5). Knowing Him as a person, His character, His ways, and the truths He wants us to know.

Victory (2:7). (NASB: "sound wisdom.") Elsewhere, this word is translated "sound judgment" (3:21, 8:14, 18:1). "In 2:7 it means success, the *result* of sound judgment."[4]

Blameless (2:7). Not sinlessness, but moral and spiritual integrity.

10. Is the mere attainment of intellectual knowledge enough for wisdom, or does wisdom require that knowledge be acted upon in daily life (2:7-8)? Why?

Optional Application: God gives victory to those who walk in integrity (2:7). Is there any sin in your life that you need to deal with?

For Thought and Discussion: How does receiving God's wisdom affect one's sense of personal well-being (2:10)?

_____

_____

_____

_____

_____

11. Many people ask, "How can I know God's will?" According to 2:1-9, what are some concrete steps to take?

_____

_____

_____

12. From 1:20-33, summarize why you should not reject wisdom.

_____

**Optional
Application:** Do you
take personal respon-
sibility for how your
life will end up? Con-
sider memorizing
1:32-33.

13. Now summarize the main message of 2:1-10.

Your response

14. What is the main way you would like to see
your life change as a result of studying
Proverbs?

If you have not already done so, read the introduction on pages 9-12.

15. As you study, you may come across difficult
concepts that you would like clarified or questions you would like answered. Jot them down
at the end of the lesson you are working on, so
that you can pursue answers later.
    If you have any questions about Proverbs
1-2 or the introduction, write them here.

For the group

This "For the group" section and the ones in later lessons are intended to suggest ways of structuring your discussions. Feel free to select what suits your group and ignore the rest. The main goals of this lesson are to begin to see what Proverbs is about and begin to know the people with whom you are going to study it.

Worship. Some groups like to begin with prayer and/or singing. Some share requests for prayer at the beginning, but leave the actual prayer until after the study. Others prefer just to chat and have refreshments awhile and then move to the study, leaving worship until the end. It is a good idea to start with at least a brief prayer for the Holy Spirit's guidance and some silence to help everyone change focus from the day's busyness to the Scripture.

Warm-up. The beginning of a new study is a good time to lay a foundation for honest sharing of ideas, to get comfortable with each other, and to encourage a sense of common purpose. So, go around the room and let each person finish these two sentences:

"One piece of wisdom my parents really tried to teach me was . . . ."

"One thing I want to get out of studying Proverbs is . . . ."

How to use this study. If the group has never used a LIFECHANGE study guide before, you might take a whole meeting to get acquainted and go over the "How to Use This Study" section on pages 5-8. Then you can take a second meeting to discuss lesson one.

Go over the parts of the "How to Use This Study" section that you think the group should especially notice. For example, point out the optional questions in the margins. These are available as group discussion questions, ideas for application, and suggestions for further study. It is unlikely that anyone will have time or desire to answer all the optional questions. A person might do one "Optional Application" for any given lesson. You might choose one or two "For Thought and

Discussion" questions for your group discussion, or you might spend all your time on the numbered questions. If someone wants to write answers to the optional questions, suggest that he use a separate notebook. It will also be helpful for discussion notes, prayer requests, answers to prayer, application plans, and so on.

Invite everyone to ask questions about how to use this guide and how your discussions will go.

Reading. It is often helpful to refresh everyone's memory by reading the passage aloud before discussing the questions. Reading all of this week's passage is probably unreasonable. So, ask someone to read 1:1-7 and someone else to read 2:1-10.

Introduction. Ask a few questions about the background material, such as,

* What is a good, short definition of "wisdom"?
* What is a proverb?
* Why were the proverbs written?

Group members don't need to memorize all of the information on pages 9-12, but that material should help them understand the background of Proverbs.

Questions. The central issues of this lesson are, "What is the fear of the Lord? Why is it essential? How is it attained?" Understanding 1:7 and 2:1-5 will lay a foundation for the rest of your study. So, concentrate your discussion around questions 3-5, 9, 12, and 13. Make sure the group leaves with a practical grasp of what a healthy fear of the Lord is. Most people have misconceptions about this idea.

Wrap-up. The group leader should have read lesson two and its "For the group" section. At this point, he or she might give a short summary of what members can expect in that lesson and the coming meeting. This is a chance to whet everyone's appetite, assign any optional questions, omit any numbered questions, or forewarn members of possible difficulties.

Encourage any members who found the overview especially difficult. Some people are better at seeing the big picture than others. Some are best at analyzing a particular verse or paragraph, while others are strongest at seeing how a passage applies to their lives. Urge members to give thanks for their own and others' strengths, and to give and request help when needed. The group is a place to learn from each other. Later lessons will draw on the gifts of close analyzers as well as overviewers and appliers, practical as well as theoretical thinkers.

Prayer. Many groups like to end with prayer. This can include prayers that respond to what you've learned in Proverbs or prayers for specific needs of group members. Some people are shy about sharing personal needs or praying aloud in groups, especially before they know the other people well. If this is true of your group, then a song and/or some silent prayer, and a short closing prayer spoken by the leader, might be an appropriate end. You could also share requests and pray in pairs.

Since 2:1-5 talks about crying out for wisdom, you might make this a focus of your prayer.

My Son

The frequent occurrence of "my son" and "my sons" in Proverbs has raised a question about Solomon's audience. There are two theories:

1. The verses in Proverbs were originally spoken orally to the *students* of Solomon's royal court.

2. The verses were originally spoken by Solomon and others to their *sons* in home settings.

Buzzell writes, "Favoring the school environment is the fact that learners were sometimes called 'sons' of their teachers. Favoring the home environment is the fact that instruction was given by mothers (1:8; 6:20; also note 23:19,22-26) as well as by fathers."[5]

---

1. *The NIV Study Bible,* edited by Kenneth Barker (Grand Rapids: Zondervan Corporation, 1985), page 946.
2. Buzzell, page 907.
3. *The American Heritage Dictionary of the English Language,* edited by William Morris (Boston: Houghton Mifflin Company, 1978), page 979.
4. Buzzell, page 910.
5. Buzzell, page 902.

Chart of Proverbs

Theme: The way to become skilled in godly living is to learn and put into practice the wisdom God provides.

		1:1-7 Prologue: The purpose and theme of Proverbs is stated.
Wisdom's Value	The Way of Wisdom Is Superior	1:8-19 Avoid bad company.
		1:20-33 Be careful not to reject wisdom.
		2 The way of wisdom has many moral benefits.
		3:1-20 Wisdom enhances every aspect of life.
		3:21-35 Wisdom involves kindness and righteousness.
		4 Wisdom is supreme.
		5 Wisdom warns against adultery.
		6:1-19 Wisdom warns about the futility of folly.
		6:20-35 Wisdom warns against sexual immorality.
		7 Wisdom warns against the enticing adulteress.
		8 Wisdom's call is issued to all mankind.
		9 Both wisdom and folly invite men to their "homes."
Solomon	Advice for Living	10-15 Solomon contrasts righteousness and wickedness.
		16–22:16 Solomon encourages godly living.
		22:17-23:35 Solomon gives advice on various practices.
		24 Solomon gives advice on various people.
		25-26 Solomon gives advice on relationships with others.
		27-29 Solomon gives advice on various activities in life.
Agur and Lemuel	Reflections	30 Agur gives observations about God and life.
		31:1-9 Lemuel speaks about God.
		31:10-31 The ideal wife is described.

PROVERBS 3:1-4:27

Wisdom's Benefits Continued

Again Solomon strives to convince his son that wisdom is worth pursuing. Ask God to impart His discernment and understanding to you, as well as a wise hunger for the knowledge that Proverbs offers.

Wisdom's value (3:1-35)

Prosperity (3:2). (NASB: "peace.") The Hebrew word *shalom* has a broad meaning and includes the ideas of wholeness, health, and harmony in life.

Love and faithfulness (3:3). (NASB: "kindness and truth.") "These are great Old Testament words which are often found linked together, for between them they express the *sine qua non* of true and lasting relations, whether between God and man, or between man and his fellow men. The *first* word (Hebrew *chesed*) expresses unswerving fidelity and constancy; the *second* expresses rock-solid integrity and trustworthiness."[1]

Acknowledge (3:6). "'Acknowledge' is quite simply 'know', which contains not only the idea of acknowledging, but the much richer content of being 'aware of', and having 'fellowship with'."[2]

Paths straight (3:6). "This means more than guidance; it means God removes the obstacles,

Solomon says that heeding wisdom yields a longer life (3:2, 9:11, 10:27, 14:27, 15:24). Do you think the longer life comes from God's direct blessing, the fact that the wise avoid danger, or both?

Optional Application: Ask God to show you how to trust Him and not lean on your own understanding.

making a smooth path or way of life, or perhaps better, bringing one to the appointed goal."[3]

1. Proverbs 3:1-10 contains five important lessons for living, each couched as a *command* and an accompanying *reward*. Summarize these using a short phrase for each.

command (3:1) _____

_____

reward (3:2) _____

_____

command (3:3) _____

_____

_____

reward (3:4) _____

_____

command (3:5-6) _____

_____

_____

reward (3:6) _____

_____

command (3:7) _____

_____

reward (3:8) _____

_____

command (3:9) _____

_____

reward (3:10) _____

_____

Do not despise . . . do not resent (3:11). Literally, "do not reject or take lightly" and "do not loathe or abhor."

2. What does God's discipline have to do with wisdom?

_____

_____

_____

_____

_____

Tree of life (3:18). A figure of speech for the source of life. It may allude to the tree in the Garden of Eden (Genesis 2:9).

3. In Hebrew, the short poem in 3:13-18 begins and ends with the same word: *blessed.* Why is wisdom worth more than silver, gold, and rubies?

_____

_____

_____

_____

_____

4. Why do you think Solomon includes 3:19-20 in this discourse on wisdom?

_____

_____

_____

_____

For Further Study: The Old Testament saints were well acquainted with the truth of Proverbs 3:5-6. How did Abraham's life testify to this truth?

For Thought and Discussion: How does God discipline His children? (You might look at Job 5:17; Psalm 38:1-22, 119:71; 1 Corinthians 11:27-32; 2 Corinthians 12:7-10; Hebrews 12:5-10.)

Optional Application: Is God using any of your current circumstances to discipline you? If so, how should you respond?

29

5. What does Solomon promise to those who hold fast to wisdom (3:23-26)?

_____

_____

_____

_____

6. Solomon often speaks of right and wrong character traits. His first list is in 3:27-32. Read this list and for each item, jot down a word or two that describes the trait Solomon says we should avoid.

3:27 _____

3:28 _____

3:29 _____

3:30 _____

3:31-32 _____

7. How would you summarize the kind of person Solomon is exhorting us to be?

_____

_____

_____

_____

_____

8. How do the three contrasts in 3:33-35 give a strong incentive to choose the right path in life?

_____

_____

_____

_____

Wisdom's supremacy (4:1-27)

9. Solomon uses intimate terms to encourage the reader to pursue a relationship with Lady Wisdom. Practically speaking, how do you think one would go about loving, prizing, and embracing wisdom (4:6,8)?

_____

_____

_____

_____

10. What are the benefits of this relationship (4:6,8-9)?

_____

_____

_____

_____

Hampered (4:12). Literally, "narrow, cramped."

11. What contrasts does Solomon draw between the "way of wisdom" and the "way of evil men" in 4:10-19?

wisdom	wickedness

For Thought and Discussion: What does it mean to guard your heart (4:23)? Why is it important?

Heart (4:21,23). "This word most commonly stands for 'mind' (e.g. 3:3; 6:32a; 7:7b; etc.; cf. Ho. 7:11), but it can go beyond this to represent the emotions (15:15,30), the will (11:20; 14:14) and the whole inner being."[4]

12. Solomon says wisdom brings health to a person's whole body (4:22). In your own words, restate his advice on using the body wisely.

heart (4:23) _____

_____

mouth and lips (4:24) _____

_____

eyes (4:25) _____

_____

feet (4:26-27) _____

_____

Your response

Chapters 3 and 4 contain many tidbits of wisdom for enhancing our lives:

- the importance of Scripture memory (3:1)
- trusting God (3:5)
- turning from sin (3:7)
- a proper attitude toward money (3:9-10)
- God's discipline (3:11-12)
- living fearlessly (3:23-26)
- love for neighbors (3:27-30)
- humility (3:34)
- avoiding bad company (4:11-19)
- disciplining the body (4:20-27)

13. Talk with God about which of the items from the list above He would like to write on your heart. Consider memorizing the relevant verses. Ask God to make you wise in this area, even if it takes discipline from Him. Jot here any

thoughts about how you would like to respond to what you've studied.

_____

_____

_____

_____

_____

14. Write down any questions you have about 3:1-4:27.

_____

_____

_____

For the group

Warm-up. To begin your discussion, go around the room and let each person briefly describe what discipline was like in his or her home growing up, and how responsive he or she was to that discipline. For instance:

"My parents were (harsh, inconsistent, firm but loving, indifferent . . .)."

"I was (a holy terror, goody-two-shoes, completely cowed, rowdy but I meant well . . .)."

Read aloud. Ask someone to read 3:1-18 aloud.

Questions. The warm-up might lead into a rousing discussion about how God disciplines us and how that might be different from what we experienced as children. Some group members may want to discuss areas of their lives where they think God is disciplining them. Ask if this is an area worth discussing.

If not, find out what issues in these chapters struck nerves in group members. Select some of the "For Thought and Discussion" questions to address those interests.

It is generally more interesting to spend your discussion on one or two thought questions that cause you to dig into the passage, than to skim over all of the numbered questions. Select just one section of the week's passage to delve into.

Don't forget to save time to ask, "So what?" How would you like what you have studied to affect your lives? How is it relevant to your circumstances?

Prayer. Ask God to enable you to grow in the areas you have studied. Let each person choose a piece of the passage to pray about: love and faithfulness, God's discipline, etc. One-sentence prayers are fine, unless your group is comfortable praying aloud and would like to pray more extensively. Close by thanking God for offering you the tree of life, the source of peace.

Jewish Education

No nation has ever set the child at center stage as did the Jews. Indeed, the child was considered the most important person in the community.[5] Rabbi Judah the Holy said, "The world exists only by the breath of school children."[6] The Jews believed that of all people, the child was dearest to the heart of God. It is accordingly no surprise that education was an extremely high priority among the Jews. Josephus wrote, "Our ground is good, and we work it to the utmost, but our chief ambition is for the education of our children."[7]

The Jews believed that the home was the absolute center of education. Schools were important to them, but the home was without parallel in its importance. Isidore Epstein asserts, "In no other religion has the duty of the parents to the children been more stressed than in Judaism."[8] Hence, the responsibility for educating the child was laid squarely on the shoulders of the parents (as in Proverbs 1:8 and 6:20).

The priority of education among the Jews is one reason why the proverbs were held in such high esteem, for they were considered to be one of the primary educational tools available. By using proverbs, parents could train their children in the art of godly living, just as their children in future years would teach the next generation the same.

1. Aitken, pages 36-37.
2. Kidner, pages 63-64.
3. Buzzell, page 911.
4. Kidner, page 68.
5. Kenneth O. Gangel and Warren S. Benson, *Christian Education: Its History and Philosophy* (Chicago: Moody Press, 1983), page 80.
6. Cited in William Barclay, *Educational Ideals in the Ancient World* (Grand Rapids: Baker Book House, 1974), page 11.
7. Josephus, *Against Apion*, 1.12.
8. Isidore Epstein, *The Jewish Way of Life* (London: n.p., 1946), cited in Barclay, page 15.

PROVERBS

The Futility of Folly

Proverbs presents us with a choice between wisdom and folly. There are three kinds of people on the path of folly: the mocker, the simple, and the fool. Solomon describes them vividly and displays the consequences of living like them in order to dissuade his son from even considering choosing their path.

For the rest of this guide, you will be jumping around Proverbs, observing its teaching on various topics rather than reading straight through the book. It is not a bad idea to first read the book through, especially chapters 5-9, which we will be largely omitting.

The mocker

1. a. According to 21:24, what is the primary trait of a "mocker" (NIV) or "scoffer" (NASB)?

   _____

   _____

   b. From what you've seen, how does mocking or scoffing reflect this trait?

   _____

   _____

   _____

For Thought and Discussion: a. How do people generally respond to mockers (24:9)?
b. How does God respond to mockers (3:34)?

Optional Application: Have you acted like a mocker recently? For the next week, be alert to times when you show this tendency. If you find that you have a problem with mocking, talk with God about how to break this pattern.

2. a. How do mockers respond to correction (15:12)?

b. What does this attitude have to do with pride?

Stir up (29:8). Literally, "fan into a flame" or "blow on embers."

3. Why do mockers inflame a city (29:8)?

4. In view of all this, how should mockers be treated, and why (22:10)?

38

The simple

5. What are two of the simple or naive person's primary problems?

14:15 _____

_____

_____

22:3 _____

_____

_____

6. Therefore, in your own words, what do you think the simple need to do? (Compare 8:5.)

_____

_____

_____

_____

_____

For Thought and Discussion: a. If the simple do not gain prudence, what can they look forward to (1:32)?
b. How can the simple gain prudence and hence escape this destiny (1:1-4)?

Optional Application: This week, watch for signs in your behavior of being simple or foolish. Talk with God about what you observe.

The fool

Despise (1:7). To hold in contempt, to belittle, to ridicule.

Chases fantasies (12:11). The Hebrew for *chase* means "to pursue frantically." *Fantasies* refers to things that are empty or worthless, either mentally or physically. In the present context, Solomon is probably referring to schemes for making quick and easy money.

Right (14:12). "*Right* means 'straight' or 'level': it is often a moral term, as in the previous verse ('upright'), but here it is a seeming shortcut to success, taken by those who are impatient of advice (cf. 12:15), or of hard work (cf. 15:19), or of moral scruples (cf. 13:14)."[1]

39

Hundred lashes (17:10). "Since no more than 40 lashes were allowed by Law (Deut. 25:2-3), this reference to 100 lashes is probably hyperbole. The wise are sensitive and learn readily, but a thickheaded fool is unresponsive even after extreme measures of correction."[2]

7. Proverbs provides us with a comprehensive list of the fool's characteristics. What do you learn about the fool's . . .

discipline (1:7)? _____

_____

_____

_____

judgment (12:11, 14:12)? _____

_____

_____

_____

temper (12:16, 29:11)? _____

_____

_____

_____

_____

ability to learn (17:10)? _____

_____

_____

focus of attention (17:24)? _____

_____

_____

8. Why do you suppose a fool would rather look to the ends of the earth to chase get-rich-quick schemes than focus on wisdom, hard work, and moral living?

_____

_____

_____

_____

_____

_____

The thorny path of folly

Ruins (19:3). Literally, "overturns" or "subverts the way."

Heart rages against the LORD (19:3). The fool blames God for his troubles.

---

9. The proverbs are clear that there are consequences for how one chooses to live. What do these passages tell you about the consequences of choosing the path of folly?

19:3 _____

_____

_____

_____

21:16 _____

_____

_____

_____

For Thought and Discussion: a. Why is it important to avoid bad company? (Consider Isaiah 52:11, John 15:19, Acts 2:40, 2 Corinthians 6:17, Ephesians 5:11, 2 Thessalonians 3:6.)
b. How do you balance this wise instruction with God's command to reach out to the ungodly with the gospel? Should we or shouldn't we be like Jesus in Luke 5:29-32?

For Thought and Discussion: What do you believe about spanking children? Do you believe in it at all? If so, how young is too young? How old is too old? What guidelines are important? Support your views biblically.

Wisdom's advice

Bear robbed of her cubs (17:12). Such bears are likely to attack with intention to kill.

10. Solomon has a lot to say about associating with fools. Paraphrase his advice in 13:20, 17:12, and 23:9.

_____

_____

_____

_____

_____

Rod (22:15). Many scholars believe this is a figure of speech representing any form of discipline.

11. a. Why is it essential that parents start dealing with children's folly from very early on (22:15)?

_____

_____

_____

_____

b. What do you think are some practical implications for parents?

_____

_____

_____

42

_____

_____

_____

Your response

12. Do a brief self-inventory by thinking about
these questions:

How do you respond when people correct you?
Are you defensive or appreciative? (9:7-8)
Do you tend to be gullible? (14:15)
Do you tend to chase dreams while ignoring
daily responsibilities? (12:11)
Do you learn lessons from life, or do you repeat
the same mistakes? (26:11)
Do those close to you say that you tend to over-
react when things go wrong? (12:16)

13. What steps can you take this week to grow in
wisdom and begin to get free of tendencies to
folly? Ask God about this.

_____

_____

_____

_____

_____

14. Write down any questions you have about this
lesson.

_____

_____

_____

_____

For the group

Warm-up. Ask each person to try to think of a time when he or she got into trouble as a young person because of naiveté. Give everyone a minute to tell his story.

Questions. The goal of this session is to help group members identify pockets of mocking, simpleness, and folly in their lives. Begin by discussing what it means to be a mocker. Ask the group to describe what a mocker does and how he thinks. What makes a person a mocker? What do you think motivates a mocker to be like that? Then ask if anyone recognized himself in the proverbs about mockers. Do you ever mock?

You can treat the topics of the simple and the fool the same way. If you've pinpointed areas in which you live in folly, take some time to discuss, "How does a person move from folly to wisdom?" Look for ways to help each other.

Prayer. Tell God about how you mock, how you are foolish, or how you are ignorant of wisdom. Ask Him to enable each of you to break your foolish habits and choose wisdom.

Wisdom Literature

Israel did not have a corner on wisdom literature in the ancient world; it was also common in Egypt, Babylon, and other countries. Egyptian examples include:

The Instruction of the Vizier Ptah-Hotep (about 2450 BC). This collection contains advice on how to be a successful state official.

The Instruction of Amen-em-Het (about 2000 BC). This contains a father's words to his son regarding how certain people he had favored disappointed him.

The Instruction of Amen-em-Ope (about 1300-900 BC). This collection contains a king's teachings to his son about various issues in life. It utilizes some words and phrases quite similar to those in Proverbs (such as "Listen my son" and "path of life").

The Babylonian collections of wisdom litera-
(continued on page 45)

44

(continued from page 44)
ture include *Counsels of Wisdom* (about 1500-1000 BC), *Akkadian Proverbs* (about 1800-1600 BC), and *The Words of Ahiqar* (about 700-400 BC). Many of the proverbs in these works are secular in nature, and some are even morally crass. The most significant difference between Proverbs and the wisdom literature of Egypt and Babylon is that the Hebrew concept of wisdom (as set forth in Proverbs) is rooted in *the fear of the Lord*. The Hebrews considered it "the beginning of knowledge." Without such fear of the Lord, no one—according to Solomon—can truly be called "wise."

1. Kidner, page 108.
2. Buzzell, page 942.

PART II

Perspectives of Wisdom

PROVERBS

God and Man

The proverbs address three questions about God and man: (1) Who is God? (2) How does God deal with man? and (3) How should man respond to God? Solomon demonstrates in pithy insights how one's commitment to wisdom reflects that person's commitment to God.

Who is God?

1. God is man's *Maker* (22:2). What does this imply about our responsibility to God? (*Optional:* See Psalm 95:6-7; Proverbs 14:31, 17:5; Isaiah 29:16; Romans 9:20.)

_____

_____

_____

_____

_____

_____

2. Solomon also calls God "the Righteous One" (Proverbs 21:12) and "the Holy One" (9:10). What difference should God's righteous and holy character make to us?

_____

For Thought and Discussion: Since God is love (1 John 4:16), how can He be said to hate anyone or anything (Proverbs 16:5)?

_____

_____

_____

_____

_____

Theologians refer to God's characteristics as *attributes.*

3. God is *omniscient.* This means He knows and comprehends everything—past, present, and future. What do you learn about God's omniscience from these proverbs?

   5:21 _____

   _____

   _____

   15:11 _____

   _____

   _____

4. God is *omnipresent.* This means He is everywhere present. What are the implications of 15:3 for your life?

   _____

   _____

   _____

   _____

   _____

5. God is *omnipotent;* He is all-powerful. What difference should 21:30 make to you?

   _____

   _____

   _____

50

_____

_____

Even the wicked (16:4). "Though this may be difficult to understand and accept, punishment for
the unrepentant is in keeping with God's justice
and is a truth frequently taught in Scripture."[1]

The lot is cast into the lap (16:33). This may refer to
the practice of holding a group of pebbles in the
fold of a garment and then shaking them to the
ground. This was a common method of making
decisions in the ancient world.

King's heart (21:1). God exercised sovereign control
over Nebuchadnezzar (Daniel 4:31-35) and
Cyrus (Isaiah 45:1-3).

Watercourse (21:1). An irrigation canal. The farmer
controlled its direction and how much water it
contained.

6. God is also *sovereign*. He is the absolute and
sole ruler of the universe. What do the following proverbs tell you about God's sovereignty?

16:4 _____

_____

_____

16:9,33; 19:21 _____

_____

_____

21:1 _____

_____

_____

7. How do you think God's sovereignty should
affect the way you live?

_____

_____

_____

_____

_____

God's dealings with man

8. God has provided His Word to ensure that man has all the knowledge he needs to enjoy proper fellowship with God. What do you learn about God's Word from 30:5-6?

_____

_____

_____

_____

Crucible . . . furnace (17:3). These were used to remove impurities from gold and silver.

Lamp of the LORD (20:27). "[A] lamp carried from room to room, and flashed into the darkest corners."[2]

9. God does not merely look upon the things men do outwardly. What else does He do?

16:2 _____

_____

_____

17:3 _____

_____

_____

20:27 _____

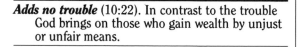

_____

_____

Adds no trouble (10:22). In contrast to the trouble God brings on those who gain wealth by unjust or unfair means.

For Thought and Discussion: What other blessings does God bestow on His children? (See 3:25-26, 10:29, 12:28.)

10. According to these proverbs, how does God deal with people?

2:7-8 _____

_____

_____

_____

10:3,22 _____

_____

_____

Man's response to God

Is kept safe (29:25). Literally, "to be inaccessibly high or exalted." The word carries the idea of being kept out of reach of danger.

11. Proverbs exhorts us to *fear* the Lord and to *trust* the Lord. Why should we fear Him?

10:27 _____

_____

_____

_____

14:26 _____

53

For Thought and Discussion:
a. Whose prayers does God hear (15:8,29)? What difference does this make to you?
    b. Proverbs 30:7-9 records a prayer of an upright man. How does this prayer reflect wisdom?

19:23 _____

12. Why should we trust Him?

3:5-6 _____

28:25 _____

29:25 _____

13. What does it mean to both fear and trust the Lord at the same time?

14. Proverbs indicates that another important responsibility believers have is to deal properly

with those people who have been offensive or unfair to them.

a. How should we respond to those who have done us wrong (20:22)?

_____

_____

_____

_____

_____

b. How should we respond to our "enemies"?

24:17-18 _____

_____

_____

_____

_____

25:21-22 _____

_____

_____

_____

_____

c. What may result for the believer who pleases God (16:7)?

_____

_____

_____

_____

Your response

15. What insight from this lesson seems most personally significant to you?

_____

_____

_____

_____

_____

16. Is there any action you would like to take in response? If so, describe it.

_____

_____

_____

_____

_____

17. List any questions you have about the proverbs in this lesson.

_____

_____

_____

_____

For the group

Warm-up. Ask group members to respond to this question: "Did you *trust* your father when you were a child? If so, what did you trust him about, and why? If not, why not?" Some members may not have had fathers present; in that case the answer is no, I didn't have a father to trust.

Most Christian counselors agree that people naturally tend to respond to God the Father the way they learned to respond to their human fathers. If they found it easy to respect and trust their earthly fathers, they will find it relatively easy to respect and trust God as Father. If they saw their human fathers as weak, passive, harsh, unpredictable, demanding, cruel, unforgiving, etc., they will find it relatively difficult to both respect and trust God. Since one of the main issues of this lesson is how to respond to God with both fear and trust, you will find it helpful to know the foundations upon which each of you is building your response to God. A flawed foundation (because of a painful childhood response to fathers) is reparable. If group members seem to have unresolved grief, hurt, fear, or resentment about their fathers, plan to take time either as a group or in private to deal with those issues. The church's age-old model for dealing with such matters is:

Confession (Here's how I felt about my father; here's how I feel now; here's what I've done in response);

Repentance (I was wrong to react in [bitterness]; I don't want to let this continue to block my relationship with God);

Forgiveness (I choose to forgive—even if I know my father was wrong; I choose to receive God's forgiveness for my own wrongdoing);

Restoration (I pray God's blessing on my father; I receive God's blessing and resurrection life for myself).

As group leader, you can help a group member through this process.

Questions. You could spend your whole time discussing what it means to both fear and trust God. Or, you could explore how to respond to each of God's attributes. Don't let your group settle for superficial answers. Help them see how God's omnipotence, sovereignty, etc., should make a radical difference in how we approach life. For instance, His love, holiness, and sovereignty mean that He really does have your lives under control. Do you believe that, or are you acting out of fear in some circumstances? Are you in a struggle for control? Again, His holiness and omniscience mean that He cares passionately about your purity and that you can't hide impurity from Him. Are you trying to hide anything from Him by hiding it from yourselves? Have you faced the fact that denial is impossible?

57

You need to be sensitive to how much probing your group can handle. Nudge them a little beyond their comfort zone. But don't push for one-time applications that won't change lives. Instead, invite group members to pray for each other about the areas they've uncovered.

Prayer. Praise God for His attributes. Ask Him to enable you to fear and trust Him, to treat Him the way He deserves to be treated because of His holiness, sovereignty, omniscience, and so on.

Proverbs in the New Testament

New Testament writers made great use of Proverbs. See how they applied the proverbs to the situations the early Christians were facing:

Proverbs 25:6-7 — Luke 14:10
Proverbs 3:7 — Romans 12:16
Proverbs 25:21-22 — Romans 12:20
Proverbs 22:9 — 2 Corinthians 9:7
Proverbs 3:11-12 — Hebrews 12:5-6
Proverbs 4:26 — Hebrews 12:13
Proverbs 3:34 — James 4:5
Proverbs 24:21 — 1 Peter 2:17
Proverbs 16:7 — 1 Peter 3:13
Proverbs 10:12 — 1 Peter 4:8
Proverbs 11:31 — 1 Peter 4:18
Proverbs 26:11 — 2 Peter 2:22

1. Buzzell, page 940.
2. Kidner, page 140.

PROVERBS

The Family

Solomon knew that God designed the family and
that each member has certain responsibilities that
help the family run smoothly. When these responsibilities are ignored, the family suffers. Therefore,
Solomon urged husbands and wives, parents and
children, to govern their relationships according to
wisdom.

Husbands and wives

1. Why do you think the man described in 27:8
   would be a troublesome husband and an inade-
   quate father?

   _____

   _____

   _____

   _____

   _____

2. A quarrelsome person is a major threat to a
   home.

   a. How is a quarrelsome man like "wood to a
      fire" (26:21)?

      _____

**Optional
Application:** Does
either 26:21 or
27:15-16 sound like
you? If so, what can
you do about it?

For Further Study:
For a fuller under-
standing of God's
ideal for husbands
and wives, see Gene-
sis 2:22-24, Ephe-
sians 5:21-33, and
1 Peter 3:1-7.

b. How is a quarrelsome woman like "a constant dripping on a rainy day" (27:15-16)?

_____

_____

_____

_____

_____

Her lamp does not go out (31:18). The noble wife plans ahead. Because of her foresight, she is worthy of praise, just as the five virgins whose lamps did not go out were praised for their foresight (Matthew 25:4).

Distaff . . . spindle (31:19). Spinning thread was a common work skill among women in the ancient Near East.

3. Proverbs 31:10-31 paints a portrait of a wife of noble character. Read this passage and make a list of her traits.

character traits _____

_____

_____

_____

_____

_____

60

mental skills _____

_____

_____

_____

_____

Optional Application: What seems to be the main quality or qualities you need to pursue in order to be God's kind of husband or wife?

practical and technical skills _____

_____

_____

_____

_____

4. What heart attitude in 31:30 is foundational to all that this godly woman does?

_____

_____

From the LORD (19:14). This phrase is emphatic in the Hebrew. "It implies that this gift is beyond both comparison and contriving."[1]

5. How does God fit into a man's pursuit of a godly wife (18:22, 19:14)?

_____

_____

_____

For Further Study: What does Scripture say about parents setting an example for their children? (See 1 Kings 9:4, 22:52; 2 Chronicles 17:3, 22:3, 26:4; Jeremiah 9:14; Amos 2:4; 2 Timothy 1:5.)

For Thought and Discussion: What do you think is the greatest threat to the family in our society? How does wisdom respond to this threat?

Parents and children

6. Restate 14:26 and 20:7 in the form of a short principle.

7. Why do you suppose a righteous lifestyle—both public and private—is the number one key to raising kids? Why is it more important than financial provision or academic advantages?

Discipline your son (19:18). This is a command in the Hebrew. It is a strong warning against being a passive parent.

Death (19:18). "Death refers either to capital punishment under the law (Deut. 21:18-21) or to the danger of natural consequences accompanying the child's foolish behavior, in which he destroys himself."[2]

Train (22:6). The Hebrew word carries the idea of "narrowing." Child-training essentially involves

62

narrowing the child's conduct away from unrighteousness and toward godliness. It involves keeping the child moving in the right direction and not getting sidetracked.

8. Solomon often speaks about the need for fathers to discipline their children (13:24; 19:18; 22:6,15; 23:13-14). According to these proverbs, why is firm discipline a crucial aspect of expressing love to children?

_____

_____

_____

_____

_____

Covers (10:12). Carries the idea of "overwhelms."

9. These proverbs were not written specifically about family relationships. Still how does each apply to relating to children, parents, and spouses?

10:12 _____

_____

_____

_____

11:17 _____

_____

_____

_____

For Further Study:
What does Solomon say about grand-parents? See 13:22 and 17:6. Living long enough to see one's grandchildren was considered a great blessing in ancient times (Genesis 48:11, Psalm 128:5-6).

For Further Study:
On wise and foolish sons, see 15:20; 17:21; 19:13; 23:15,24-25; 29:3.

13:10 _____

_____

_____

_____

_____

15:18 _____

_____

_____

_____

_____

20:22 _____

_____

_____

_____

10. What light do your answers to question 9 shed on how to carry out discipline in a godly manner? (That is, do the proverbs in question 9 justify stern, cold, demanding discipline?)

_____

_____

_____

_____

_____

Will be pecked out (30:17). The Israelites considered the loss of an eye to be a terrible and loathe-some curse. (Compare Judges 16:21.)

11. a. What kinds of children cause shame to their parents?

10:5 _____

_____

28:7 _____

_____

30:17 _____

_____

b. What counsel does Proverbs give for avoiding such traits in children? (Recall 19:18, 20:7, 22:6.)

_____

_____

_____

_____

Optional Application: Talk to God about the areas in which you fall short as a parent, child, or spouse. Tell Him exactly how you feel about your situation. Tell Him both your pain and your sin. Ask Him for the grace to be the kind of person Proverbs describes. Ask Him for the grace to rely on His grace rather than on your own ability to try harder.

Your response

12. What have you learned in this lesson that might help you in your relationships with . . .

your spouse? _____

_____

_____

_____

your children? _____

_____

_____

_____

your parents? _____

_____

_____

_____

_____

others with whom you relate? _____

_____

_____

_____

_____

13. What steps can you take to begin putting these
insights into practice this week?

_____

_____

_____

_____

_____

_____

14. List any questions you have about the proverbs
in this lesson.

_____

_____

_____

For the group

Warm-up. Ask group members, "What was one thing
you learned about marriage (good or bad, wise or
foolish) from your parents?"

Questions. Try to discern whether your group will

benefit most from discussing husbands and wives or parents and children. If you have singles in your group, male-female relations are probably still relevant, and the character qualities are worth pursuing even if one doesn't have a mate.

Don't let the discussion stay on a theoretical level. Use the marginal questions: Is anyone in the group willing to admit to a quarrelsome streak? Is anyone willing to say that he or she is angry at his or her spouse for not being the Proverbs 31 woman or for being the 27:8 man? How could your marriage be better if *you* (not your spouse) became more like what you saw in question 9?

Or, if you are discussing parenting, what is the biggest challenge each parent in the group is experiencing? How do each of you need to grow in godliness in order to deal with your kids? (Parents tend to want to focus on what's wrong with their kids, but Proverbs stresses that parents should give the most attention to their own character.) How could *your* becoming more like what you observed in question 9 improve the situation in your home?

Prayer. Tell God about how you fall short as family members. Thank Him that His grace is available to make you into the kinds of people Solomon praises. Ask for that grace to be real and powerful in one another's lives.

1. Kidner, page 133.
2. Buzzell, page 947.

PROVERBS

Friendship

Solomon was rich and famous, yet he needed real friends as much as an unknown poor man. God made man with a built-in need and capacity for companionship. And through Solomon, He provides us with rich insights for making our friendships as fulfilling as possible in a sinful, fallen world.

Quality or quantity

1. What do you think Solomon is trying to say in 18:24?

_____

_____

_____

_____

2. In your own words, what do you think 14:20 and 19:4 are saying?

_____

_____

_____

_____

_____

For Further Study:
Look at some biblical examples of close friendships (Ruth 1; 1 Samuel 18:1-4, 19:1-7, 20:1-42; Matthew 27:55-56; Romans 16:3-4; 2 Timothy 1:16).

For Further Study:
How does it feel to be abandoned and friendless? See what happened to the psalmists and Jesus, and how they responded (Psalm 31:6-13, 38:8-12, 88:6-9, 142:1-7; Mark 14:50-72; John 21:15-19).

a. What do you think parents should do if they disapprove of their children's friends?

b. What criteria should determine where to "draw the line" regarding acceptable and unacceptable friends for one's children?

c. What should parents say to a child who claims he or she has no friends?

d. If you are dissatisfied with the quantity or quality of your children's friendships, take a look at the example you are setting. Have you modeled the kinds of healthy relationships you'd like your children to have? Have you been a good friend to your children, your spouse, and others? Talk with God about how you can improve the model you are giving your children.

3. Does this mean one should seek wealth in order to accumulate friends? Why or why not? (Consider 18:24.)

_____

_____

_____

_____

_____

Cautious (12:26). This Hebrew word carries the idea of one who "searches out" or "investigates." (NIV translates this sentence, "A righteous man is cautious in friendship," while NASB renders it as, "The righteous is a guide to his neighbor.")

4. Why is it important to be cautious in choosing friends (12:26)? See, for instance, 2:20-22.

_____

_____

_____

_____

Whom to avoid

Hot-tempered man (22:24). Literally, "an owner or possessor of anger."

5. In each of the following passages, Solomon says it is wise to avoid certain kinds of people. He also tells us why we should avoid them. Paraphrase his advice in your own words.

20:19
whom to avoid _____

reason why _____

22:24-25
whom to avoid _____

reason why _____

23:6-8
whom to avoid _____

reason why _____

Pride (13:10). Pride or presumption "is stated to be an ingredient in every quarrel; not, that is, in every difference of opinion, but in the clash of competing and unyielding personalities."[1]

Firebrands (26:18). Firebrands can easily ignite sheaves of grain.

6. Solomon speaks about other negative character traits that make a person undesirable as a friend. Summarize each of these traits in a few words.

13:10 _____

_____

_____

15:18 _____

_____

_____

16:28 _____

_____

_____

18:1 _____

_____

_____

25:19 _____

_____

_____

25:20 _____

_____

_____

26:18-19 _____

_____

_____

26:21 _____

_____

_____

Good friend

Close friends (17:9). This is a single word in Hebrew and denotes "bosom companions."

7. From these proverbs, describe the qualities Solomon considers to be important in good friends.

11:13 _____

_____

_____

17:9 _____

_____

_____

17:17 _____

_____

_____

19:11 _____

_____

_____

20:3 _____

_____

_____

22:11 _____

_____

_____

27:9 _____

_____

_____

For Thought and Discussion: What do you think it means to "cover over an offense" (17:9)? Can you think of any examples of this?

For Thought and Discussion: a. Do you think it is realistic to expect anyone but Jesus to be a perfect friend, as described in question 7? Why or why not?
b. What should you do when your human friends fall short of perfection?

For Thought and Discussion: The Scriptures describe Moses, Abraham, and the apostles as friends of God. What qualities would you have to have in order to be a good friend to God?

73

For Further Study:
Have you ever been betrayed by a friend? If you are still feeling the effects, see Job 19:13-29, Psalm 41:9-13, Matthew 26:47-56, and 2 Timothy 4:14-17.

Seldom (25:17). "Literally, 'make precious,' that is, 'make it valuable' by its rarity. A person should refrain from frequently visiting his neighbor, to avoid being a nuisance, but he should visit enough so that his visits are valued."[2]

8. It takes effort to keep a friendship healthy. What do you learn about friendship maintenance from these proverbs?

3:27-28 _____

_____

_____

17:14 _____

_____

_____

25:17 _____

_____

_____

Wounds (27:6). Probably inner hurts that come from being rebuked or criticized.

9. What do you think Solomon is saying in 27:6?

_____

_____

_____

74

10. Why do you think friends are sometimes more valuable than relatives in times of distress (27:10)?

_____

_____

_____

_____

_____

11. What implications does 27:17 have in regard to friendship?

_____

_____

_____

_____

Optional Application: If you feel you don't have enough friends, focus on how to become a better friend to others. Which qualities in question 7 do you lack? How can you grow in these?

Optional Application: Do any of the negative traits in questions 5 and 6 damage your friendships? If so, why do you suppose you are like that? What steps can you take to begin shedding those habits?

A good name

Bind them . . . write them (3:3-4). These are "striking expressions for glorying in, meditating on and (7:3) acting by these principles."[3]

12. How valuable is a good name (22:1)?

_____

_____

13. Why do you think a good reputation is so important?

_____

_____

14. How does Solomon advise us to attain a good name?

3:3-4 _____

_____

_____

_____

25:9-10 _____

_____

_____

_____

Your response

15. What is the most significant insight you've had during this lesson about wise living?

_____

_____

_____

_____

_____

16. How would you like what you've learned to affect your life?

_____

_____

_____

_____

17. Are there any steps you can take to pursue this effect?

_____

_____

_____

_____

_____

18. List any questions you have about this lesson.

_____

_____

_____

For the group

Warm-up. Ask, "When you were in grade school, did you have many or few friends? How did you feel about that?"

Questions. Instead of going through the questions as written, try this structure:
Is quality or quantity most important in friendship? Why?
What kinds of people does Solomon say make poor friends, and why?
What are the qualities of a good friend?
What is hard for you about being or having friends?
How can each of us grow in being good friends? What practical steps can we take?

Prayer. Tell God about the ways in which you fall short as friends and about the frustrations you have about your friendships. Ask Him for wisdom in dealing with your friendships, and ask Him to mature you in the positive traits of good friends.

1. Kidner, page 102.
2. Buzzell, page 961.
3. Kidner, page 63.

PROVERBS

Sexual Purity

Times have changed, but people haven't. Ever since
the Fall, mankind has struggled with sexual purity.
The problem is catastrophic in modern Western
society, so Solomon's wisdom in this area is all the
more relevant.

By heeding wisdom's voice, Solomon says, a
person can avoid disaster and enjoy life as it was
meant to be. But each person must choose for himself which path he will take—wisdom or folly. Especially with regard to sex, this choice is a life-or-
death issue.

Seduction

1. Read 7:6-27. How does this young man demonstrate a lack of sound judgment (7:7-9)?

   _____

   _____

   _____

   _____

Crafty intent (7:10). Literally, "secretive in heart."

Fellowship offerings (7:14). (NASB: "peace offering.") "Portions of the sacrificial animal were

79

taken home by the offerer. Without refrigeration the meat had to be consumed; so a feast usually accompanied the sacrifice."[1]

Today I have fulfilled my vows (7:14). According to Leviticus 7:15-16, the meat from a vowed fellowship offering had to be eaten on the first or second day.

2. What are some of the primary characteristics of the adulteress (7:10-12)?

_____

_____

_____

_____

Honey . . . oil (5:3). Honey was considered the sweetest substance in ancient Israel, and oil was considered the smoothest. Here, honey is a metaphor for pleasant-sounding talk, or possibly for kisses. Oil suggests words that are soothing and flattering.

3. What is the adulteress's strategy (5:3, 7:21)?

_____

_____

_____

_____

4. The adulteress is clearly the aggressor in 7:6-27. Does this mean that the naive young man is innocent? Why or why not?

_____

_____

_____

_____

_____

5. Proverbs doesn't talk about men seducing naive women because the book is addressed to sons rather than daughters. How do you think 7:6-27 applies to women?

For Further Study: Scripture often addresses the problem of lust. What does God say about lust in Matthew 5:27-30, Galatians 5:16-18, Colossians 3:5, 1 Thessalonians 4:5-8?

_____

_____

_____

_____

_____

6. How is the unthinking young man like an ox or a bird (7:22-23)?

_____

_____

_____

7. Why do you think yielding to the adulteress leads to death (7:22-27)?

_____

_____

_____

_____

_____

For Further Study:
Read Samson's story in Judges 14–16. In what ways is Samson an example of what happens to the sexually impure?

Reduces you to a loaf of bread (6:26). The services of a professional prostitute are expensive and ultimately reduce a man to poverty.

8. What else will happen to a person who commits adultery?

5:7-14 _____

_____

_____

_____

6:25-26 _____

_____

_____

_____

6:30-35 _____

_____

_____

_____

9. Proverbs 6:27-29 states the principle that underlies all of what you've read. Put it into your own words.

_____

_____

_____

_____

_____

Saved by wisdom

10. A simple person walks naively into a situation that will draw him or her into adultery. How

82

does a prudent person deal with a situation that threatens to overwhelm him or her emotionally (27:12)?

_____

_____

_____

Your own cistern . . . your own well (5:15). "As a person would not get water from his neighbor's cistern because he had his own (2 Kings 18:31), so a man should have his physical needs met by his own wife, not someone else's."[2]

In the public squares (5:16). An unfaithful husband may cause his wife to become promiscuous.

Captivated (5:19). (NASB: "exhilarated.") Literally, "intoxicated."

_____

Optional Application: a. What should one do if he falls into sin (28:13)? b. Are you afraid to face any sin in your life because you believe God can't or won't forgive and cleanse it? If so, remind yourself that it is pride to believe that any sin of yours is too big for God to handle. Confess your sin to God, and believe that He is able to provide the grace to resist that sin.

11. Read 5:15-23. What is Solomon getting at with the figures of speech in 5:15-17?

_____

_____

_____

_____

_____

12. Solomon says a man should be so *intoxicated* by love and sex with his wife that he won't be drawn to other women (5:19). How could this happen for an ordinary couple?

_____

_____

_____

_____

83

Your response

"If you want to avoid the devil, stay away from his neighborhood. If you suspect you might be vulnerable to a particular sin, take steps to avoid it."[3]

13. How does the above quotation (and its parallel in 4:25,27) apply to you? Consider:
    the kinds of people you see socially;
    the relationships you have with members
        of the opposite sex at your workplace;
    the magazines and books you read;
    the movies you watch;
    the television shows you watch.

_____

_____

_____

_____

_____

14. Is there anything else in this lesson that you want to take to heart? If so, write it down.

_____

_____

_____

_____

15. List any questions you have about this lesson.

_____

_____

_____

_____

For the group

Warm-up. Ask, "Have you ever gotten into a morally compromising situation by not thinking ahead, perhaps when you were a teenager?" Let anyone who feels comfortable doing so describe what happened.

Questions. Case studies help groups come to grips with how biblical teaching applies in today's real situations. Here are some circumstances you might discuss:

Would you drive to another city (maybe three or four hours) alone with a person of the opposite sex other than your spouse? Why or why not?

Would you have a business meeting alone with a person of the opposite sex behind a closed door? Why or why not?

If you were married, would you meet a friend of the opposite sex alone for lunch? Why or why not?

Would your answers to any of these questions change if you knew the other person was attracted to you?

How would you apply Solomon's advice to single people dating and having friends?

Prayer. Ask God to give each of you discernment in the situations in which you find yourselves. If any group members have specific dilemmas they are struggling with, pray about those.

1. Buzzell, page 920.
2. Buzzell, page 915.
3. Robert L. Alden, *Proverbs: A Commentary on an Ancient Book of Timeless Advice* (Grand Rapids: Baker Book House, 1983), page 63.

PROVERBS

The Blessings of Righteousness

Solomon often equates the path of wisdom with the path of righteousness, and the path of folly with the path of wickedness. He insists, contrary to what most people believe, that ethical, God-centered living is ultimately wiser than self-centered living. Is he right?

Righteous (10:6). In right relationship to God and the community, as defined by the covenant given by God. To be righteous, a person did not need to be morally perfect. Rather, he simply needed to be doing his best to live God's way. This included personal devotion to God, faith in His promises, moral integrity, and offering sacrifices for sin. God regarded Abraham as having fulfilled his covenant requirements when he simply believed God's promise (Genesis 15:6). David called himself righteous (Psalm 18:24)—even though he sinned severely—because he fulfilled God's covenant requirements of confession, humility, trust in God's mercy, and sincere desire to become a holy person.

Under the new covenant, which Jesus inaugurated, a person is in right relationship to God if he puts his faith in Jesus. That is, his confidence of being accepted by God is not in what he is able to do, but in what Jesus has done (dying for sins and rising from death) and is doing (transforming His people into holy

Optional Application: Do you act as though your standing with God depends on how faithful you are to pray, study the Bible, do good things, treat people well, succeed in ministry, or some other standard of performance? Take a close look at your heart about this. Ask God to convince you that you stand because of His commitment to you and Jesus' finished work, not on your commitment to Him.

people). His primary loyalty is to Jesus, his master.

It is very important not to misunderstand *righteous* as meaning "morally perfect by one's own efforts." This error leads to legalism, pride, and despair.

Straight way (11:5). A life with fewer obstacles and troubles that hinder one from attaining one's goals.

Light . . . lamp (13:9). Figures of speech representing physical life.

Shines brightly (13:9). A figure for personal satisfaction, joy, and prosperity.

---

1. What does Solomon expect for the righteous?

2:7-8 _____

_____

10:3 _____

_____

11:5 _____

_____

11:28 _____

_____

13:9 _____

_____

21:21 _____

_____

Trouble (22:8). (NASB: "vanity.") Emptiness, futility.

Rod of his fury (22:8). The wicked person's ability to oppress the innocent through manipulative techniques.

88

Bold (28:1). "The straightforward man, like the lion, has no need to look over his shoulder. What is at his heels is not his past (Nu. 32:33) but his rearguard: God's goodness and mercy (Ps. 23:6)."[1]

2. What does Solomon promise to the wicked?

21:12 _____

22:5 _____

22:8 _____

26:27 _____

28:1 _____

3. From what you've seen of the world, does experience appear to support or refute the idea that the righteous are blessed and the wicked will suffer? Explain.

_____

_____

_____

_____

4. What would happen to faith, hope, and sacrificial love if righteousness always paid off in this life? (You might consider the accusation Satan makes about Job in Job 1:9-11.)

_____

_____

Optional Application: Do you wonder if you are suffering because you are wicked or for some other reason? Talk with God about this. If He doesn't convict you of some specific wrongdoing, have confidence that your suffering is not punishment. Don't let Satan weigh you down with false guilt. On the other hand, if God does convict you, confess and turn from your sin.

_____

_____

_____

Blessed are his children (20:7). "His children, seeing his example of integrity, are encouraged to be the same kind of people."[2]

5. How do the righteous affect people around them?

10:7 _____

_____

20:7 _____

_____

23:24 _____

_____

6. Why do you suppose it is better to be righteous and poor than wicked and rich (16:8, 19:1, 28:6)?

_____

_____

_____

_____

7. Offering sacrifices to God was one of the most important aspects of Old Testament worship. Yet why do you suppose righteousness is even more important than such formal religious services (21:3,27)?

_____

_____

90

_____

_____

_____

8. Why is righteousness essential for good government (16:12; 20:26; 28:15,28; 29:2,12)?

For Thought and Discussion: Do the proverbs in question 8 address any moral problems in the government of your country?

_____

_____

_____

_____

Your response

9. What aspect of this study most motivates you to pursue righteousness?

_____

_____

_____

_____

10. Ask the Lord what aspect of righteousness He would like you to concentrate on this week. Perhaps it has something to do with what you have studied during the past few weeks. Perhaps you need to focus on cultivating a more intimate, trusting relationship with Him—a righteousness not based on your ability to succeed and perform. Write your plans here.

_____

_____

_____

_____

11. List any questions you have about this lesson.

_____

_____

_____

_____

For the group

Warm-up. Ask each person to rate his current circumstances on a scale of 1 to 10, where 1 equals intense suffering and 10 equals fabulous prosperity.

Questions. The two key points your group should get from this lesson are: (1) what righteousness is and isn't, and (2) why Proverbs says the righteous prosper and the wicked suffer.

On the first point, ask group members to define righteousness in their own words. Be sensitive to subtle legalism. It's hard to shake the idea that we are righteous if we demonstrate serious commitment to God through certain acts. We need to see that our commitment is frail, but that we stand because God stays committed to us. The righteous are those who are confident in God's commitment to them. Their godly deeds are a response of gratitude for the relationship they receive freely.

On the second point, many people feel that experience shows wicked people prospering and righteous people suffering. The books of Job and Ecclesiastes agree that it often looks that way. But Proverbs asserts that if you look at whole lives, more often than not the wicked end up miserable and the righteous end up joyful, even if they are poor and sick. What do you think?

Consider also the case of Job. Satan charged that Job was righteous in order to earn blessing from God. God afflicted Job to prove that Job was godly out of sheer love, not manipulative selfishness. How does this put your own circumstances into perspective? Do your group members feel cheated if they suffer when they are good? This is a sure sign that they are operating on selfishness, not love, and that they think they earn blessings rather than receive them as gracious gifts.

Prayer. Thank God for the blessings you each receive as the natural consequences of righteous living. Praise Him that He is worthy of your love even when He allows you to suffer in a fallen world. Praise Him for His love and justice.

1. Kidner, page 168.
2. Buzzell, page 948.

LESSON NINE

PROVERBS

Humility Versus Pride

It is impossible, says Solomon, for one to be committed to the way of wisdom and at the same time
manifest selfish pride. These are mutually contra-
dictory. Why? Let's see.

Choices and consequences

Proud (18:12). Literally, "to be high." The word can
mean "exalted" or "haughty."
Pride is regarding oneself as the most
important person around. It is the belief that
feeling loved and significant depends on being
above others. It may manifest either in *too high*
or *too low* self-esteem—either way it is an
obsession with one's own value.
Humility, by contrast, is finding one's
worth so securely in God's unearned favor that
one is not very concerned about self-esteem at
all. A humble person doesn't put himself down,
avoid compliments, or play the martyr. His sta-
tus compared to others doesn't matter much to
him because his value in God's eyes is a settled
issue.

1. Read 16:18, 18:12, and 22:4.

a. Why is pride foolish?

For Thought and Discussion: Can you think of any events in your own life that demonstrate what you wrote for question 1?

For Further Study:
a. How do Uzziah and Herod illustrate pride that leads to destruction (2 Chronicles 26:16-18, Acts 12:21-23)?
   b. Other examples of pride include Naaman (2 Kings 5:11), Hezekiah (2 Chronicles 32:25), Haman (Esther 3:5), Nebuchadnezzar (Daniel 4:30), and Belshazzar (Daniel 5:23). Do any of these remind you of yourself?

b. Why is humility wise?

_____

_____

_____

_____

_____

2. What do you learn about the meaning of humility from two of the men God honored most—David and Paul?

2 Samuel 7:18-21 _____

_____

_____

_____

_____

1 Timothy 1:15-16 _____

_____

_____

_____

_____

Six . . . seven (6:16). A Hebrew idiom indicating that the list is specific but not exhaustive.

3. Proverbs 6:16-19 lists seven things God hates. The first and foremost is haughtiness. Why do you think God detests pride so much?

_____

_____

_____

_____

_____

The many faces of pride

It's no good, it's no good (20:14). Buyers and sellers bargained over the price of each item under consideration. The buyer sometimes questioned the quality of the item in order to drive the price down further.

Clouds and wind without rain (25:14). "Clouds and wind usually give farmers promise of rain. But if no rain comes, the farmers are keenly disappointed."[1]

4. Pride can be exhibited in many ways. How do the people in each of the following proverbs display pride?

13:7 _____

_____

18:2 _____

_____

18:11 _____

_____

18:19 _____

_____

20:14 _____

_____

25:14 _____

_____

5. Can you see any signs of pride—a focus on how important or valued you are, on how you look or what people think—in your life? Talk with God about this, and write down any thoughts.

_____

_____

_____

_____

_____

_____

6. a. Solomon urges his son, "do not be wise in your own eyes" (3:7). What is Solomon's evaluation of such a person (26:12)?

_____

_____

_____

b. How can you tell whether you are wise in your own eyes? How does it show?

_____

_____

_____

_____

7. What is the humble way to interact with others (25:27, 27:2)?

_____

_____

98

_____

_____

_____

Your response

8. What do you think a person can do to grow freer of pride? (Consider the meaning of pride.)

_____

_____

_____

_____

_____

_____

9. Consider your answers to questions 5 and 8. Are there any steps you want to take?

_____

_____

_____

_____

_____

_____

10. List any questions you have about this lesson.

_____

_____

_____

_____

_____

Optional Application: What in this lesson motivates you to resist the temptation to brag about accomplishments?

Optional Application: Ask God to enable you to deal with the areas in your life in which pride is evident. Ask Him to help you develop humility in all you say and do. Give Him permission to do whatever it takes to give you the humility of being secure in Him, no matter what people think.

For the group

Warm-up. Many people find it tough to detect pride in themselves. Often the most proud people are honestly unaware of their pride because they have made such an effort to hide it from themselves. People who feel contempt for themselves rarely realize that this contempt reflects a proud belief that their deficiencies make them, alone of all humanity, unlovable to God.

Therefore, your goal in this lesson should be to help your group members recognize pride in themselves and learn how to grow free from it. As a warm-up question, try asking each person to define pride in his or her own words.

Questions. With the aid of questions 2 through 4, try to come to a useful description of pride. What is the root of pride? How does it manifest in actions? Then discuss how a person attains humility. How do you become so secure in God's attitude toward you that you aren't preoccupied with self-worth anymore?

Prayer. Ask God to so ground you in the knowledge of His love for you that pride ceases to be an issue with you. Pray for new security and selflessness in the areas of your lives where you can see pride.

1. Buzzell, page 960.

PROVERBS

Hard Work Versus Laziness

Solomon had quite a sense of humor when it came to describing sluggards. His goal, of course, was to prod his students into committing themselves unreservedly to a lifestyle of diligence.

The sluggard

A little . . . a little . . . a little (24:33). "All he [the sluggard] knows is his delicious drowsiness; all he asks is a little respite. . . . He does not commit himself to a refusal, but deceives himself by the smallness of his surrenders. So, by inches and minutes, his opportunity slips away."[1]

1. Read Proverbs 24:30-34. How does Solomon argue from "effect" to "cause" in these verses?

_____

_____

_____

_____

_____

For Thought and Discussion: Read how Solomon describes those who love sleep (6:4,9-10; 10:5; 20:13; 23:21). Do you have any problems in this area?

2. Restate 24:32-34 in the form of a short principle.

_____

_____

_____

_____

In season (20:4). (NASB: "After the autumn.") The season for plowing and planting in the Middle East is the winter, the rainy season. Hence, farmers must plow in muddy fields and in the cold.

3. Read 20:4. What would be a modern parallel to the man who goes hungry because he won't plow during the unpleasant conditions of winter?

_____

_____

_____

_____

_____

4. Why is the sluggard's way of life such a frustrating existence (21:25)?

_____

_____

_____

_____

5. What quality of life does the sluggard have to put up with as a result of his laziness (15:19)? (What do thorns suggest to you?)

102

_____

_____

_____

_____

_____

For Further Study:
On making excuses, see Exodus 3:11, 4:10; Judges 6:15; Jeremiah 1:6-7; Matthew 25:24-25; and Luke 14:18-20 in context. Is this a problem for you?

Lion (22:13). "Most probably a lion (cf. 26:13) would not be roaming the streets of an Israelite town."² The excuse is obviously absurd.

6. Read 22:13. Name one excuse you have heard (or given yourself) for getting out of work.

_____

_____

_____

_____

7. In your experience, how do sluggards show themselves to be "wise in their own eyes" (26:16)?

_____

_____

_____

_____

8. What do you think Solomon is teaching about the sluggard by calling him "vinegar to the teeth and smoke to the eyes" (10:26)?

_____

_____

Optional
Application: Are you
tempted by get-rich-
quick schemes? If so,
why?

9. What does the sluggard desperately need to learn from the ant (6:6-9)?

Contrasting lifestyles

Chase fantasies (28:19). Probably a reference to schemes for making quick and easy money.

10. Solomon draws many contrasts between the lazy man and the diligent man. Some of these are found in the following references. In the left column, write the word or phrase from each verse that characterizes the lazy man. In the right column, write the word or phrase that characterizes the diligent worker.

the lazy man	the diligent worker
10:4	
10:5	

	the lazy man	the diligent worker
20:13		
28:19		

For Thought and Discussion: a. Do you think welfare programs foster laziness? Why or why not?
    b. If you do, how would you suggest that society avoid the laziness problem while caring in a biblical manner for the poor?

For Further Study: For a fuller grasp of the virtue of hard work, see Genesis 2:2-3,15; Ecclesiastes 5:18-20; Mark 6:3; Acts 18:3; 1 Thessalonians 4:11-12; 2 Thessalonians 3:10; and Revelation 14:13.

Brother (18:9). A figure of speech for "similar."

Skilled (22:29). The Hebrew word for "skilled" can mean "quick" or "prompt." The word is closely related to "diligence."

11. What is Solomon teaching by his description of the lazy man in 18:9?

_____

_____

_____

_____

_____

12. In contrast to the lazy man, what do you learn about the diligent man who applies himself to his work (22:29)?

_____

_____

_____

_____

Optional Application: If you are aware of something in you that drives you either to overwork or avoid work, take time to talk with God about it. Confess any sin you identify. Ask God what steps you can take to become more godly in this area.

Your response

13. Solomon is extremely critical of resting. But God's command to work for six days and rest on the seventh (Exodus 20:8-11) puts Solomon's teaching into its full biblical perspective. From that passage and what you've seen in Proverbs, what would you say is a healthy attitude about work and rest?

_____

_____

_____

_____

_____

_____

14. Are you more tempted to work constantly and find yourself unable to rest? Or are you more tempted to find excuses not to work? Or are you a combination of both?

_____

_____

_____

_____

_____

15. How is what you've learned in this lesson relevant to your life?

_____

_____

_____

_____

_____

16. What response would you like to make to what you've learned?

17. List any questions you have about this lesson.

_____

_____

_____

_____

For the group

Warm-up. Let each person respond briefly to this question: "Do you see yourself more as someone who tends to (1) work too hard; (2) avoid working hard; or (3) be in balance about work and rest?"

Questions. It doesn't take much to figure out that Solomon's basic thesis is: "Don't be a lazy bum." Bring your group beyond that to explore why people are lazy or workaholic. What are the heart-level sins and false beliefs that produce these behaviors? And how does a person repent of and break free from those heart-level sins?

Prayer. Tell God about your struggles with godly attitudes toward work. Ask Him to strengthen you to acquire and act on biblical attitudes so that your lives will show a healthy balance between work and rest.

1. Kidner, page 42.
2. Buzzell, page 954.

PROVERBS

Proper Speech

Solomon has a great deal to say about what we say! The almost 150 references to the tongue, lips, mouth, etc., indicate that proper speech is one of his top priorities. The tongue, says Solomon, can accomplish great good if used for wisdom, but severe damage if used foolishly. Accordingly, Solomon offers his observations to guide us in the wise approach.

Destruction versus healing

1. How is a "word aptly spoken" like apples of gold in settings of silver (25:11)?

_____

_____

_____

_____

2. What do you think Solomon means when he refers to pleasant words as a "honeycomb" (16:24)?

_____

_____

_____

_____

For Thought and Discussion: How is meddling in someone's quarrel like seizing a dog by the ears (26:17)?

For Further Study: Just how powerful is the tongue (James 3:1-6)?

For Thought and Discussion: Why is it often hard to speak encouragement?

For Further Study:
Examples of encouraging words are in Exodus 14:13; Isaiah 41:13; Matthew 9:2, 14:27, 17:7; Acts 23:11, and 27:22. If you desire to become more encouraging, ponder these examples this week, and look for chances to encourage someone.

Gentle (15:1). Literally, "soft."

Harsh (15:1). Literally, "hurtful."

Deceitful (15:4). (NASB: "perversion.") The word depicts something twisted or turned away from normal.

3. Solomon repeatedly emphasizes that the tongue can be a destructive or a healing force. Below, write down words and phrases that depict the tongue as healing or destructive.

	destructive force	healing force
12:18		
15:1		
15:4		

4. What can encouragement achieve (12:25)?

Lying versus truth-telling

Honest answer (24:26). Literally, "upright or straight words."

Seven (26:25). This number symbolized perfection or completeness to the Hebrews. The point here is "lots and lots."

For Thought and Discussion: Is it ever right to lie? What about Corrie ten Boom, who lied to the Nazis that no Jews were hidden in her house? What about Exodus 1:15-22 and Joshua 2:1-7?

5. Proverbs 6:16-19 lists seven things God hates. Which three involve the tongue?

_____

_____

_____

6. a. What common cause of lying does 26:24-26 point out?

_____

_____

b. Why is this worth remembering?

_____

_____

_____

_____

7. How does Solomon describe honest speaking in 24:26?

_____

_____

_____

_____

_____

Gossip

Gossip (11:13). Literally, "one who goes about in slander." Gossip is talking about someone who isn't present when (if one were honest with oneself) the motive is self-centered rather than to build someone up in love. Slander is saying negative things about someone who isn't present. Thus, slander is a subset of gossip. It is slander whether or not the information is true.

We tend to justify gossip and slander with righteous motives (asking a friend to pray for the person, making sure that necessary people are properly informed about the person, and so on). Because gossip is so ingrained and the excuses are so easy and subtle, it's a good idea to ask yourself some straight questions about information you want to share:

Does this person *really* need to know in order to prevent harm or build someone up in love?

What is the potential hurt to the people being discussed?

What is my *real* reason for passing this along? Is it love for the person discussed and for the hearer?

8. What is wrong with repeating things told to you in confidence (17:9)?

_____

_____

_____

_____

_____

9. Solomon says keeping confidences is a sign of being "trustworthy" or faithful (11:13). How would he treat you if he found you unfaithful in this matter (20:18)?

_____

_____

10. Many people devour gossip (18:8). What do you suppose happens to a person who listens to gossip and thereby lets it go into his inmost parts?

_____

_____

_____

_____

For Further Study: If you have trouble with flattery, meditate on these examples: 2 Samuel 14:17, Daniel 11:21, Luke 20:21, Acts 12:22.

Flattery

Flatters (29:5). Literally, "makes [a person] smooth." The word *flattery* carries the idea of "smooth talk that deceives."

11. What does Solomon mean in 29:5 when he says that "whoever flatters his neighbor is spreading a net for his feet"? Why is this so?

_____

_____

_____

_____

12. Sometimes it is hard to muster the nerve to rebuke people who need it. What important insight does Solomon offer in regard to this in 28:23?

_____

_____

_____

For Thought and Discussion: a. How can fools put on the mask of wisdom (17:28)?
b. Do you think this is a good thing to do? Why or why not?

For Thought and Discussion: What do you think it means to guard one's mouth (13:3, 21:23)?

Wisdom's restraint

13. Why is it foolish to speak too soon (18:13)?

_____

_____

_____

_____

_____

Even-tempered (17:27). Literally, "cool of spirit." A modern parallel would be to "keep one's cool."

14. Why is it wise to keep your cool and restrain your mouth (10:19, 17:27)?

_____

_____

_____

_____

_____

Weighs (15:28). Carries the idea of "carefully muses or meditates on."

Guides his mouth (16:23). Literally, "causes his mouth to be prudent."

15. What is the relationship between a righteous person's heart and his words (15:28, 16:23)?

_____

114

_____

_____

_____

16. When should you *not* restrain your tongue (31:8-9)?

_____

_____

_____

_____

Your response

17. Spend a few minutes giving thought to your present speaking habits. Evaluate yourself in the following areas by writing "never," "rarely," "more than rarely," or "often" next to each item.

lying (including "white lies") _____

gossiping _____

boasting _____

flattering _____

profanities _____

quarreling _____

mocking _____

talking too much _____

questionable jokes _____

stinging remarks in anger _____

Talk with God about areas where you need to grow. Confess any sin to Him, and thank Him for His forgiveness and for the power that is available from Him to change. Ask Him to begin working on you in the areas you've mentioned.

For Further Study: Why is proper speech essential, according to Matthew 12:35-37 and James 2:12-13?

Optional Application: Do you know anyone who is presently going through tough times? If so, make an effort to encourage him or her with a kind word. Solomon says this is one of the tongue's best uses.

18. Is there any other action you want to take?

_____

_____

_____

_____

_____

19. List any questions you have about this lesson.

_____

_____

_____

_____

For the group

Warm-up. Ask, "What's the nicest thing someone has said to you during the past week?"

Questions. If necessary, omit some of the questions so that you have enough time to deal with areas in which you each want to grow. First, discuss how one becomes more godly in using one's tongue. What is God's part? What is your part?

Then divide into groups of three, and let each person tell the other two what use of the tongue he or she most wants to grow in (truthfulness, encouragement, confidence-keeping, clean language, cool temper, gentleness). Discuss what each of you could do to cooperate with God in this matter. Finally, pray for each other to have the insight and ability to turn away from wrong habits toward right ones. Ask God to deal with the things in your hearts that motivate wrong use of your mouths.

Prayer. Talk with God about how you each use your tongues. Tell Him what you find tough, and ask for the strength to pay attention to what you say and the power to change. Pray for each other about issues raised during your discussion.

PROVERBS

Emotions

Solomon seems to have experienced the whole range of emotion from agonizing depression to ecstatic joy. Through that experience, he gained much wisdom about emotions and how to deal with them.

Happiness versus heartache

Crushed (18:14). Literally, "stricken" or "prostrated."

1. Solomon says that the wise man gives attention to his emotional state. Why?

   15:13 _____

   _____

   _____

   17:22 _____

   _____

   _____

   18:14 _____

   _____

For Thought and Discussion: Can a person who is laughing outwardly be depressed on the inside? See 14:13. Why is this important to know?

For Further Study: A day is coming when all sorrow will be banished. See Isaiah 25:8, 35:10, 51:11, 60:20, 65:19; Jeremiah 31:12; Revelation 7:17, and 21:4.

For Further Study: Sin leads to depression. How does Psalm 51:8-12 reflect this truth?

For Further Study:
Did Jesus experience
joy while on earth?
Start with John 15:11
and Hebrews 12:2,
then look through the
Gospels for evidence
one way or the other.

**Optional
Application:** What
attitudes in your heart
hinder you from living
joyfully?

2. How are righteousness and joy related (10:28,
29:6)?

_____

_____

_____

_____

_____

Peace (12:20). "Peace includes the idea of general
welfare—and to be planning this for other
people is to enjoy its by-products ourselves."[1]

3. What are some things that Solomon says add
joy to life?

11:10 _____

_____

_____

12:20 _____

_____

_____

15:30 _____

_____

_____

21:15 _____

_____

_____

23:24 _____

_____

_____

Contentment versus envy

4. Restate 14:30 in your own words.

_____

_____

_____

_____

_____

_____

5. It is sometimes difficult for the righteous (who are honest and just in their dealings) to watch the wicked get ahead in life by dishonest and unjust means. Why does Solomon say the righteous should not envy such people (24:19-20)?

_____

_____

_____

_____

_____

6. What is Solomon's secret of contentment (19:23)?

_____

_____

_____

_____

_____

Patience versus a quick temper

Displays (14:29). Literally, "to exalt or lift up for show."

For Further Study:
How should your hope for the future affect your emotional state (Psalm 37:37; Proverbs 11:7, 23:18; Jeremiah 29:11).

For Further Study:
On contentment, see Luke 3:14, Philippians 4:11, 1 Timothy 6:6-8, and Hebrews 13:5.

For Thought and Discussion: How does one calm an angry situation (15:1)?

For Thought and Discussion: How does drinking alcohol affect the emotions (23:29-30)?

7. Why does a quick temper show folly (14:29)?

_____

_____

_____

_____

Whose walls are broken down (25:28). Without walls, a city was completely vulnerable to enemy attacks. The ancients also considered broken walls to be a disgrace.

8. How is a man who lacks self-control "like a city whose walls are broken down" (25:28)?

_____

_____

_____

_____

Jealousy

9. What do you think Solomon is getting at in his question in 27:4?

_____

_____

_____

_____

Your response

Galatians 5:16-23 says that joy, peace, patience, and the control of emotions are fruits of living purposely under the influence of God's Spirit. Talk with God about how you can do this more fully.

120

10. In what area of your emotions would you most like to see growth?

_____

_____

_____

_____

_____

11. What can you do to cooperate with God's Spirit in this area?

_____

_____

_____

_____

12. List any questions you have about this lesson.

_____

_____

_____

For the group

Warm-up. Ask everyone to respond to this question: "Do you consider yourself to be a joyful Christian? Why or why not?"

Questions. The proverbs on emotions deal chiefly with how to maintain joy. Joy is supposed to be a fruit of walking with God, yet it eludes many Christians. Solomon implies that righteousness, contentment, patience, and other character qualities are essential to having consistent joy.

It's easy for these proverbs to seem like platitudes. So, take an honest look at yourselves. What aspects of your attitudes toward God and others tend to rob you of joy?

Some Christians believe they have to pretend to be "up" all of the time in order to be a good witness for Christ. Do you agree? Do you feel safe being honest with the others in your group about your emotions, even if those emotions reveal that you fall short of sainthood? If you sense a tendency in your group to wear emotional masks, have a talk about honesty. Why is or isn't your group a safe place to be real?

Prayer. Pray for each other regarding your areas of emotional weakness. Ask God to deal with your tempers, or your jealousy, or your discontentment. Ask Him to bring joy to one another's lives by uprooting the sources of joylessness and by enabling you each to live according to His Spirit.

Wesley on Joy

John Wesley, the founder of Methodism, believed that joy was an essential ingredient of the holy life. Christians who are joyful about their relationship with the Lord have little trouble maintaining their commitment. Conversely, those who are discouraged or depressed are more likely to fall into sin. "Consequently," wrote Wesley, "whatever dampens our joy in the Lord proportionally obstructs our holiness."[2] This is why Satan so often attempts to rob Christians of their joyful relationship with the Lord. If he can dampen their joy, he can undermine their commitment to God and so make it much easier to lead them into sin.

---

1. Kidner, page 98.
2. John Wesley, *The Nature of the Kingdom* (Minneapolis: Bethany House, 1979), page 33.

PROVERBS

Wealth and Poverty

How fitting it is that Solomon—the richest man in the world of his time—act as our advisor on matters of money. From Solomon's wise advice, we can discern many principles related to priorities and attitudes in dealing with poverty and wealth. And how relevant his advice is in a time when materialism consumes even Christians. Best of all, Solomon's advice is free.

For Thought and Discussion: How might poverty be a blessing in disguise (13:8)?

Fine tuning your priorities

Fattened calf (15:17). The ancients considered this meat a luxury and generally reserved it for special occasions.

Poor . . . blameless (28:6). Or, "destitute" and "morally whole."

1. Although Solomon acknowledges that material wealth has benefits, he is quick to point out that it must be kept in proper perspective. Certain things have a higher priority. Solomon communicates some of these priorities with comparative proverbs couched in "better is . . . than . . ." format.

    Read the following proverbs and summarize them in the appropriate columns on the next page.

better is	than
15:16	
15:17	
16:8	
17:1	
28:6	

2. What conclusions do you draw from these contrasts?

_____

_____

_____

_____

_____

_____

The road to poverty

Wine and oil (21:17). These were considered extrav-
agances associated with lavish feasting.

---

3. Solomon offers many insights on why some
   people end up in poverty. What reasons do you
   find in these verses?

   14:23 _____

   _____

   _____

   20:13 _____

   _____

   _____

   21:5 _____

   _____

   _____

   21:17 _____

   _____

   _____

   23:21 _____

   _____

   _____

   28:19 _____

   _____

   _____

Optional Application: Do any of the habits in question 3 sound like your lifestyle?

For Further Study:
a. On borrowing money, see Exodus 22:14, 2 Kings 6:5, and Psalm 37:21.
  b. What is Jesus' teaching on loaning money (Luke 6:30-38)?

For Thought and Discussion: What do you think of credit cards, in light of Solomon's counsel?

Optional Application: What steps can you take to be debt free by this time next year (or two years from now if you are in bad shape)?

4. What does Solomon mean by his statement in 22:7 about borrowing money?

_____

_____

_____

_____

_____

_____

Strikes hands in pledge (22:26). When taking out a loan, a person had to put up some kind of collateral to guarantee that he would pay it back. The deal was sealed by striking hands (similar to our handshake).

You could also pledge security for someone else's loan. If he defaulted, you would have to pay the debt.

5. What is the danger in taking out loans (22:26-27)?

_____

_____

_____

_____

_____

Solomon also says that cosigning on someone else's loan is sheer madness (6:1-5). The point is that if you can't afford to loan money to a friend and never see a penny back, then you can't afford to cosign his loan (since you are promising to pay in the very real possibility that he won't). You are also risking losing your friend as well as your property.

126

Insights on prosperity

Accurate weights (11:1). "To increase their profits many merchants used two sets of stone weights when weighing merchandise. Lighter stones were placed on the scales when selling (so that a lesser quantity was sold for the stated price), and heavier ones were used when buying (so that more was obtained for the same price). With the absence of coinage, scales were used in most daily commercial transactions."[1]

6. Why should these proverbs motivate you to flee from making money dishonestly?

11:1 _____

   _____

   _____

   _____

20:17 _____

   _____

   _____

   _____

Blessing of the LORD (10:22). The Hebrew adds an emphatic pronoun: "The blessing of the Lord— *it* makes one rich." The implication is that nothing but God's blessing makes one truly rich.[2]

Adds no trouble to it (10:22). God stands against those who make money dishonestly, but "adds no trouble" to those whom He blesses with wealth.

For Thought and Discussion: Prosperity theology teaches that "whom the Lord loveth, the Lord maketh rich." Do you agree? Why or why not? Specifically:
a. Is wealth necessarily a sign of God's favor?
b. Is poverty necessarily a sign of God's disfavor?
c. Does God want all Christians to be rich?
d. Should we be praying to get rich?

For Further Study: What do Deuteronomy 8:11-20 and 1 Samuel 2:7-8 say about the true source of wealth? How should these passages affect your attitudes?

7. What insights do you gain from the following passages regarding the relationship of . . .

wisdom and prosperity (8:18-21)?

_____

_____

_____

_____

God's blessing and prosperity (10:22)?

_____

_____

_____

hard work and prosperity (10:4)? _____

_____

_____

_____

saving money and prosperity (13:11)?

_____

_____

_____

_____

Kindness to the poor

8. How does one's attitude toward the poor reflect one's relationship with God (14:31, 19:17)?

_____

_____

_____

9. How do these proverbs motivate us to respond to the needs of the poor, rather than pretending they don't exist?

21:13 _____

_____

_____

28:27 _____

_____

_____

For Thought and Discussion: Should believers be involved in social reform to help the poor (29:7, 31:8-9)? Specifically, how do you think we should put this into practice?

Optional Application: a. Do you think your church adequately hears the cries of the poor?
   b. How can you respond to the needs of the poor?

Fine tuning your attitudes

Day of wrath (11:4). A reference either to the future day of judgment or to death.

Stingy man (28:22). Literally, "man with an evil eye."

Greedy (28:25). Literally, "large of soul," referring to an uncontrolled and avaricious appetite for material things.

10. We've seen Solomon's exhortations to work hard. But what does he say about getting rich by . . .

overworking (23:4-5)? _____

_____

_____

_____

_____

For Thought and Discussion: What do you think of Agur's attitude toward wealth in 30:7-9? Why do you feel that way?

stinginess (28:22)? _____

_____

_____

_____

_____

greed (28:25)? _____

_____

_____

_____

_____

11. Why shouldn't the pursuit of wealth be one's top priority (11:4)?

_____

_____

_____

_____

12. Why is generosity wiser than stinginess (11:24-25, 22:9)?

_____

_____

_____

_____

_____

Your response

13. What aspect of this lesson seems most personally relevant to you?

_____

_____

_____

_____

_____

14. How would you like this to affect your life?

Optional Application: Read a practical Christian book on handling finances, such as *Master Your Money* by Ron Blue.

_____

_____

_____

_____

15. What step can you take toward this end?

_____

_____

_____

_____

16. List any questions you have about this lesson.

_____

_____

_____

_____

For the group

Warm-up. Ask group members to tell one question or concern about finances they are currently facing.

Questions. As you go through the questions in this lesson, keep summarizing what you learn as a list of basic principles of handling money. Have someone in the group write those principles down, then read them back at the end of your discussion. Then let each person tell which principle he or she most needs to work on applying. You might talk about what makes it hard to live by some of the principles. Finally, come up with some concrete ways to begin putting the principles you've named into practice. Help each other see possible strategies.

Prayer. Thank God for giving you so much wise guidance in handling money. Ask Him for the strength, courage, and unselfishness to live by His principles. Tell Him about the areas in which you fall short. Ask for His forgiveness and the grace to change.

1. Buzzell, page 928.
2. Kidner, page 88.

PROVERBS

Life and Death

Whether one chooses to travel the way of wisdom or the way of folly is literally a life-or-death decision.

Folly and death

Complacency (1:32). Carries the idea of a false sense of security.

1. A primary theme in Proverbs is that folly leads to death. In each of the following proverbs, what is the aspect of folly that leads to death?

   1:32 _____

   _____

   5:22-23 _____

   _____

   10:21 _____

   15:10 _____

2. Why do you think these things lead to *death*?

   _____

   _____

For Thought and Discussion: a. If people really faced the fact that they are going to die one day soon, how do you think that would affect their behavior?
b. Why do you suppose people refuse to face this fact?

For Thought and Discussion: a. What is the relationship between longevity and obedience to God? See 1 Kings 3:14, Job 5:26, Psalm 91:16, Isaiah 65:22, Zechariah 8:4, and 1 Peter 3:10.
b. What is the relationship between health and obedience to God (Exodus 15:26, Deuteronomy 7:15, Jeremiah 30:17)?
c. Does this mean that everyone who dies young or gets sick does so because of some specific, personal sin? Why or why not?

Without remedy (6:15). "Whether natural consequences or more direct divine intervention is in view is not clear. But his downfall is quick, complete, and certain."[1]

3. It often looks as though the wicked are getting away with their evil scot-free. Why isn't this really true (6:15, 29:1)?

_____

_____

_____

_____

_____

Wisdom and life

Crown of splendor (16:31). The ancients held the elderly in high honor. Gray hair was accordingly considered something to be proud of.

4. How does the way of wisdom affect longevity (9:10-11, 10:27, 16:31)?

_____

_____

_____

_____

_____

_____

Bones (3:8). A Hebrew metaphor representing the whole body.

5. How does the way of wisdom relate to bodily health (3:7-8, 4:20-22)?

_____

_____

_____

_____

Eternal concerns

6. What do you think "boast about tomorrow" means in 27:1? Give an example or two of what this might look like in modern life.

_____

_____

_____

_____

_____

7. Why is it foolish to boast about tomorrow?

_____

_____

_____

_____

8. Solomon says God exercises sovereign control over both life and death (16:9, 19:21). How is this both a comfort and a threat?

_____

For Thought and Discussion: Should we pray for a long life? Why or why not?

For Further Study: Compare Proverbs 27:1 to Luke 12:16-21.

For Thought and Discussion: How do you reconcile God's sovereignty with human free will and responsibility?

For Thought and Discussion: Do you have an eternal hope? If it is not solid, read 1 Peter 1:3-12 and Revelation 21:1-22:5. How would your life be different if the prospect of eternity really gripped your understanding?

For Further Study: How does Paul characterize death in 1 Corinthians 15:26? What is God's solution?

_____

_____

_____

9. How should this fact affect our lives?

_____

_____

_____

_____

_____

Wrath (11:23). Probably a reference to judgment.

Immortality (12:28). Literally, "no death." Until after Jesus' resurrection, God didn't give His people a very clear idea of what "no death" might look like.

_____

10. What does Solomon say about the hopes of the righteous and the wicked after this life?

the wicked (11:7,23; 24:19-20) _____

_____

_____

the righteous (12:28, 14:32) _____

_____

_____

Comfort the dying

Beer . . . wine (31:6). These were used as anesthetics or drugs to deaden physical pain and deep emotional bitterness.

11. What do you think 31:6-7 says about comforting the dying?

_____

_____

_____

_____

_____

Optional Application: Are you using the brief time you have on earth for the maximum benefit to God's Kingdom? How can you treat your life as a precious trust?

12. What implications might this passage have for modern medicine?

_____

_____

_____

_____

_____

Your response

13. How has this lesson comforted you and/or issued you a warning?

_____

_____

_____

_____

_____

14. How would you like to respond?

_____

_____

_____

_____

15. List any questions you have about this lesson.

For the group

Warm-up. Ask, "Would you say you are living an abundant life? Why or why not?"

Questions. It's been said, "Fear not that you will die; fear rather that you will never really live." Discuss the implications of this piece of advice. What does it mean to "really live," according to biblical standards? What can one do to really live? How do Jesus Christ and the Holy Spirit make an abundant life possible? How does Satan try to keep you from really living?

Make sure to bring this discussion down to the realm of the practical. Come up with some concrete steps you can each take in the pursuit of real life.

Prayer. Thank God for showing you the way to life. Give Him permission to do whatever it takes to bring you into real life on this earth, making a real contribution to His work in the world.

1. Buzzell, page 917.

CHALLENGE AND REVIEW
Looking Back

1. We have seen that wisdom essentially involves *skill in the art of godly living*, and that this skill relates to every area of life. By leafing back through what you have written, summarize what you have learned from Solomon about the following. Use a sentence or two for each.

the way of wisdom _____

_____

_____

_____

_____

_____

_____

the way of folly _____

_____

_____

_____

_____

_____

man's proper response to God ——————————————

——————————————

——————————————

——————————————

——————————————

——————————————

husbands and wives ——————————————

——————————————

——————————————

——————————————

——————————————

parents and children ——————————————

——————————————

——————————————

——————————————

——————————————

friendship ——————————————

——————————————

——————————————

——————————————

——————————————

sexual purity ——————————————

——————————————

——————————————

righteousness _____

humility and pride _____

hard work and laziness _____

wealth and poverty _____

_____

_____

_____

_____

_____

2. Have you noticed any areas of your life (attitudes, thoughts, relationships with people, habits) in which you have already changed as a result of studying Proverbs? If so, explain.

_____

_____

_____

_____

_____

_____

3. Look back over the "Your response" section in each chapter. Are you satisfied with how you have followed through on the personal applications you wanted to make? Take some time to pray about those areas you think you should continue to pursue. What can you do to continue sharpening your skills in the art of godly living?

_____

_____

_____

_____

_____

4. Do you have any questions about Proverbs that remain unanswered? If so, some of the sources on pages 145-146 may help you answer those questions. Or you might want to study some particular passage with cross-references on your own. Write your unanswered questions here.

_____

_____

_____

_____

_____

For the group

Compare notes on your answers to question 1. Spend at least twenty minutes discussing how you've changed and how you would still like to change. It's been said that it takes six months to develop a new habit; are there any habits you would like to practice for the next six months? How can you encourage each other in doing so?

Evaluation. Take a few minutes or a whole meeting to assess how your group functioned during your study of Proverbs. Some questions to consider are:

What did you learn about small group study?

How well did the study help you grasp Proverbs?

What were the most important truths you discovered about the Lord?

What did you like best about your meetings?

What did you like least? What would you change?

How well did you meet the goals you set at your first meeting?

What are members' current needs? What will you do next?

Prayer. Thank God for all you've learned from studying Proverbs together. Thank Him for the ways He has worked in each of your lives. Ask Him to show you what areas of your lives He wants to work on next, and ask Him to encourage each of you as He does so. Pray about any specific desires for application you discussed during this meeting.

STUDY AIDS

For further information on the material covered in this study, consider the following sources. If your local bookstore does not have them, you can have the bookstore order them from the publisher, or you can find them in most seminary libraries. Many university and public libraries will also carry these books.

Commentaries on Proverbs

Aitken, Kenneth T. *Proverbs* (The Daily Study Bible Series, The Westminster Press, 1986).
  Aitken's book is a handy topical reference guide to Proverbs. The book is divided into three sections: (1) Types of Characters; (2) Wisdom in Various Settings; and (3) Ways of Man and the Ways of God. Under each major section are studies of relevant subtopics. This is an excellent tool for the layperson.

Alden, Robert L. *Proverbs: A Commentary on an Ancient Book of Timeless Advice* (Baker Book House, 1983).
  A good introductory study to the book of Proverbs, with many applicational and devotional insights. A helpful overview.

Buzzell, Sid S. "Proverbs" in *The Bible Knowledge Commentary* (Victor Books, 1985).
  This is one of the best verse-by-verse commentaries on Proverbs. It has an excellent introductory section, and it is especially good on word meanings and the culture of the day. It is scholarly yet readable for laypeople.

Ironside, Henry Allen. *Notes on the Book of Proverbs* (Loizeaux Brothers, n.d.).

145

A classic study on Proverbs. This book has been around for a very long time but is still in print. Ironside offers commentary on every verse and often provides helpful illustrations. The book is highly devotional and applicational.

Jensen, Irving L. *Proverbs* (Everyman's Bible Commentary, Moody Press, 1982).

A good structural study of Proverbs. Includes helpful charts. The book is in outline format and focuses on the "big ideas" within the overall structure of Proverbs. The book is not intended as a verse-by-verse commentary.

Kidner, Derek. *The Proverbs: An Introduction and Commentary* (Tyndale Old Testament Commentaries, InterVarsity Press, 1964).

The introduction of this book is especially helpful, providing valuable background material for understanding Proverbs. Following the introduction is a section entitled "Subject Studies" in which Kidner briefly outlines what Proverbs says about major themes in the book. The commentary itself is quite brief and is less helpful than the preceding sections.

Histories, Concordances, Dictionaries, and Handbooks

A *history* or *survey* traces Israel's history from beginning to end, so that you can see where each biblical event fits. *A Survey of Israel's History* by Leon Wood (Zondervan, 1970) is a good basic introduction for laymen from a conservative viewpoint. Not critical or heavily learned, but not simplistic. Many other good histories are available.

A *concordance* lists words of the Bible alphabetically along with each verse in which the word appears. It lets you do your own word studies. An *exhaustive* concordance lists every word used in a given translation, while an *abridged* or *complete* concordance omits either some words, some occurrences of the word, or both.

The two best exhaustive concordances are *Strong's Exhaustive Concordance* and *Young's Analytical Concordance to the Bible*. Both are available based on the King James Version of the Bible and the New American Standard Bible. *Strong's* has an index by which you can find out which Greek or Hebrew word is used in a given English verse. *Young's* breaks up each English word it translates. However, neither concordance requires knowledge of the original language.

Among other good, but less expensive concordances, *Cruden's Complete Concordance* is keyed to the King James Version and Revised Versions of the Bible, and *The NIV Complete Concordance* is keyed to the New International Version. These include all references to every word included, but they omit "minor" words. They also lack indexes to the original languages.

A ***Bible dictionary*** or ***Bible encyclopedia*** alphabetically lists articles about people, places, doctrines, important words, customs, and geography of the Bible.

The New Bible Dictionary, edited by J. D. Douglas, F. F. Bruce, J. I. Packer, N. Hillyer, D. Guthrie, A. R. Millard, and D. J. Wiseman (Tyndale, 1982) is more comprehensive than most dictionaries. Its 1300 pages include quantities of information along with excellent maps, charts, diagrams, and an index for cross-referencing.

Unger's Bible Dictionary by Merrill F. Unger (Moody, 1979) is equally good and is available in an inexpensive paperback edition.

The Zondervan Pictorial Encyclopedia edited by Merrill C. Tenney (Zondervan, 1975, 1976) is excellent and exhaustive, and is being revised and updated. However, it is made up of five 1000-page volumes. Because of the financial investment, all but very serious students may prefer to use it at a library.

Unlike a Bible dictionary in the above sense, *Vine's Expository Dictionary of New Testament Words* by W. E. Vine (various publishers) alphabetically lists major words used in the King James Version and defines each New Testament Greek word that KJV translates with that English word. *Vine's* lists verse references where that Greek word appears, so that you can do your own cross-references and word studies without knowing any Greek.

Vine's is a good basic book for beginners, but it is much less complete than other Greek helps for English speakers. More serious students might prefer *The New International Dictionary of New Testament Theology*, edited by Colin Brown (Zondervan) or *The Theological Dictionary of the New Testament* by Gerhard Kittel and Gerhard Friedrich, abridged in one volume by Geoffrey W. Bromiley (Eerdmans).

A ***Bible atlas*** can be a great aid to understanding what is going on in a book of the Bible and how geography affected events. Here are a few good choices:

The Macmillan Atlas by Yohanan Aharoni and Michael Avi-Yonah (Macmillan, 1968, 1977) contains 264 maps, 89 photos, and 12 graphics. The many maps of individual events portray battles, movements of people, and changing boundaries in detail.

The New Bible Atlas by J. J. Bimson and J. P. Kane (Tyndale, 1985) has 73 maps, 34 photos, and 34 graphics. Its evangelical perspective, concise and helpful text, and excellent research make it a very good choice, but its greatest strength is its outstanding graphics, such as cross-sections of the Dead Sea.

The Bible Mapbook by Simon Jenkins (Lion, 1984) is much shorter and less expensive than most other atlases, so it offers a good first taste of the usefulness of maps. It contains 91 simple maps, very little text, and 20 graphics. Some of the graphics are computer-generated and intriguing.

The Moody Atlas of Bible Lands by Barry J. Beitzel (Moody, 1984) is scholarly, very evangelical, and full of theological text, indexes, and references. This admirable reference work will be too deep and costly for some, but Beitzel shows vividly how God prepared the land of Israel perfectly for the acts of salvation He was going to accomplish in it.

A **handbook** of biblical customs can also be useful. Some good ones are *Today's Handbook of Bible Times and Customs* by William L. Coleman (Bethany, 1984) and the less detailed *Daily Life in Bible Times* (Nelson, 1982).

For Small Group Leaders

The Small Group Leader's Handbook by Steve Barker et al. (InterVarsity, 1982).
Written by an InterVarsity small group with college students primarily in mind. It includes information on small group dynamics and how to lead in light of them, and many ideas for worship, building community, and outreach. It has a good chapter on doing inductive Bible study.

Getting Together: A Guide for Good Groups by Em Griffin (InterVarsity, 1982).
Applies to all kinds of groups, not just Bible studies. From his own experience, Griffin draws deep insights into why people join groups; how people relate to each other; and principles of leadership, decision making, and discussions. It is fun to read, but its 229 pages will take more time than the above book.

You Can Start a Bible Study Group by Gladys Hunt (Harold Shaw, 1984).
Builds on Hunt's thirty years of experience leading groups. This book is wonderfully focused on God's enabling. It is both clear and applicable for Bible study groups of all kinds.

How to Build a Small Groups Ministry by Neal F. McBride (NavPress, 1994).
This hands-on workbook for pastors and lay leaders includes everything you need to know to develop a plan that fits your unique church. Through basic principles, case studies, and worksheets, McBride leads you through twelve logical steps for organizing and administering a small groups ministry.

How to Lead Small Groups by Neal F. McBride (NavPress, 1990).
Covers leadership skills for all kinds of small groups—Bible study, fellowship, task, and support groups. Filled with step-by-step guidance and practical exercises to help you grasp the critical aspects of small group leadership and dynamics.

DJ Plus, a special section in *Discipleship Journal* (NavPress, bimonthly).
Unique. Three pages of this feature are packed with practical ideas for small groups. Writers discuss what they are currently doing as small group members and leaders. To subscribe, write to Subscription Services, Post Office Box 54470, Boulder, Colorado 80323-4470.

Bible Study Methods

Braga, James. *How to Study the Bible* (Multnomah, 1982).
Clear chapters on a variety of approaches to Bible study: synthetic, geographical, cultural, historical, doctrinal, practical, and so on. Designed to help the ordinary person without seminary training to use these approaches.

Fee, Gordon, and Douglas Stuart. *How to Read the Bible For All Its Worth* (Zondervan, 1982).
After explaining in general what interpretation (exegesis) and application (hermneneutics) are, Fee and Stuart offer chapters on interpreting and applying the different kinds of writing in the Bible: Epistles, Gospels, Old Testament Law, Old Testament narrative, the Prophets, Psalms, Wisdom, and Revelation. Fee and Stuart also suggest good commentaries on each biblical book. They write as evangelical scholars who personally recognize Scripture as God's Word for their daily lives.

Jensen, Irving L. *Independent Bible Study* (Moody, 1963), and *Enjoy Your Bible* (Moody, 1962).
The former is a comprehensive introduction to the inductive Bible study method, especially the use of synthetic charts. The latter is a simpler introduction to the subject.

Wald, Oletta. *The Joy of Discovery in Bible Study* (Augsburg, 1975).
Wald focuses on issues such as how to observe all that is in a text, how to ask questions of a text, how to use grammar and passage structure to see the writer's point, and so on. Very helpful on these subjects.

Titles in the LifeChange series: